LIVE TO

NEVER LOSE

AGAIN

LIVE TO

NEVER LOSE

AGAIN

Finding you, inside you.

JARVIS BUCHANAN

Copyright © 2023 Jarvis Buchanan

All rights reserved. No part of this publication may be reproduced, distributed, or transmitted in any form or by any means, including photocopying, recording, or other mechanical methods, without the prior written consent of the publisher, except in the case of brief quotations embodied in critical reviews and certain other noncommercial uses permitted by copyright law. For permission requests, contact the author at the website listed below.

Jarvis Buchanan

www.ldrpsy.com

Dedicated to those who want to overcome adversity,
and embrace inner power through positivity.

Acknowledgment

First, let me thank God for giving me the determination and strength to complete this book. His guidance and tutelage, through my individual experiences, has been instrumental in helping me understand the inner workings of my own life in a way that supports my expression and advice to you. Next, to my loving family, I appreciate you allowing me the time, energy, and space to delve into my passion. It is our experiences that helped to shape "Live to Never Lose Again" and those same experiences are now highlighted as a beacon of light to those who are facing their darkest times. These experiences, quite possibly, are the last accountable stand between those who are at the crossroads of giving up on the most precious gift of all, life, or pivoting to a glimmer of faith that this book offers in the form of hope, power, and focus. I am thankful to the network of people, throughout my life, who have impacted me in any way. I believe that it took the entire network of my relationships and connections to bring me to this moment, and I salute you for creating the human that can now withstand the storms of life and pass along the lessons, in the form of guidance to others.

Lastly, a special thank you to Janki Thakkar for her amazing developmental editing, copy editing, and proofreading. Her expert opinion added refreshing recommendations to my content and elevated high points for easier comprehension and flow.

Preface

Being in a leadership position in an occupation, relationship, or community often makes you an uncertified personal counselor. In my case, as an officer in the military, my opportunities were most prevalent during the time I commanded military units. It makes you responsible for the training, supply, maintenance, and most importantly, morale and welfare of each soldier under your authority. Unfortunately, during my second command, we lost a soldier to suicide. Although, I could not have changed the soldier's decision, I took the loss of his life personally. After a grievance period, I studied and became much more aware of the "dark times" that not only soldiers, but people at large go through. Since that time, I vowed to use my experience and education to help as many people as possible to overcome suicidal thoughts and tendencies. *Live to Never Lose Again* is the beginning of a much larger initiative of my company, LeadershiPsych, that builds on the principles of this book and takes what you learned to the next level. If you are interested in exploring my work further, please visit www.ldrpsy.com.

Introduction

Is this book for you? There are several how-to strategies, processes, and anecdotes to help you build the perfect life. On many occasions, some are helpful, while others are schemes and frauds that prey on a vulnerable psyche. This book is different. It promotes a perspective that will help "you" never lose again by helping "you" understand "yourself" in conjunction with all the conditions that made "you" possible. Yes, this book is all about... guess who? "You." It will not give you a cookie-cutter solution for your specific problem, because each of us is different in our own ways, but the content has been designed to guide you through a series of moments, using the blueprints that life has offered as your guide. These are your moments, and you must decide, each second, what you will do with the next. People are always consciously, as well as subconsciously, making critical life decisions. My job is to slow "you" down and help you recognize what is going on behind the scenes in your life, so that you can better control the narrative of your future.

Over time, many lessons learned are fragments of wisdom, which, when put together, form strong, intelligent, successful, and considerate people. However, the fragments are not always easy to put together so that they can be viewed as a whole, because life's happenings, along with our conditioning, convince us to focus on the negativity in our lives. Thus, we rarely get the opportunity to see ourselves as the heroes of our life stories. I will help you identify and use the algorithm that transforms your thoughts from constantly focusing on negativity to understanding that all "things" lead to positivity. Please understand that by no means is the book trying to understate the significance of whatever is going on in your life. On the contrary, the intent is to allow you to thrive in your temporary situations by focusing on the wholeness of your essence and the beauty of your future. The change in thought pattern is how you consistently "live to never lose again."

I enjoy studying people and reading extensively, but I do not attribute every example in this book to a source or reference, because I like to think for myself and develop my own conclusions based on my understanding of the world. I recommend you adapt that perspective too. What I am offering you is decades of experience while dealing with people, observing them, making mistakes, and noticing the sets of common circumstances that form the basis of inferences to help you either avoid a certain behavior, fix specific habits, or at the very least, understand your options when facing life decisions.

It is not my plan to sit you on a notional sofa and dissect your way of thinking. However, I invite you, if you see fit, to recline and let this book take you in the direction you need it to take you, at this point in your life. I am just a normal guy, who wants to help normal people to feel what they consider to be normal again. Honestly, the way to understand that is through a true dive into your definition of "normal," but we will get into that if you decide to keep reading, which I hope you do.

If you belong to the group of millions, if not billions, of people, who are searching for answers about who you are, your purpose, and why you cannot seem to get it together, read this book. If you have already found your formula to never lose again, pass the book to a friend who may not be so lucky. I believe it will help. This book has not been written to heal you. Rather, it has been written to give you tools to heal yourself.

Contents

1. Letting Go...1
   a. Needs and Agendas..2
   b. Identifying the Need..10
   c. Your Environment 14
   d. Finally Letting Go 16

2. Validation...19
   a. External Validation...20
   b. Self-Validation 24
   c. Self-Evaluation 27
   d. The Internal Struggle 33

3. Confront the "L" (Loss or Lesson)................................39
   a. Good Grief..40
   b. Adversity...42
   c. The Grief Process 43

4. Your Passion...51
   a. Quid Pro Quo 52
   b. What Is Your P assion?......................................55
   c. Answering the Call 57
   d. Discovery 60
   e. Identifying Your Passion....................................65

5. Life Cycles 71
   a. Behind the Scenes...72
   b. Categories..77
   c. Storms of Life..80

xiii

6. The Intangibles...87
   a. Focus..88
   b. Belief...90
   c. The Psychology of Focus...........................93
   d. Breakthrough......................................100
   e. Rhythm..102

7. Balance...105
   a. What is Important?................................106
   b. Priorities..108
   c. Willpower...111
   d. Planning..114
   e. Then, Now, Later..................................118
   f. Distractions......................................122

8. Connections...127
   a. Law of Attraction.................................128
   b. Misconception.....................................130
   c. Higgs Boson.......................................131
   d. Applied Conditioning..............................134
   e. Types of Connection...............................136

9. Power...141
   a. The Algorithm.....................................142
   b. Common Types of Power.............................145
   c. Power and Karma...................................148
   d. Vignettes: Examples of Power Plays................152

Paul Laurence Dunbar—1872

Keep A-Pluggin' Away.

I've a humble little motto
That is homely, though it's true, —
Keep a-pluggin' away.
It's a thing when I've an object
That I always try to do, —
Keep a-pluggin' away.
When you've rising storms to quell,
When opposing waters swell,
It will never fail to tell, —
Keep a-pluggin' away.

If the hills are high before
And the paths are hard to climb,
Keep a-pluggin' away.
And remember that successes
Come to him who bides his time, —
Keep a-pluggin' away.
From the greatest to the least,
None are from the rule released.
Be thou toiler, poet, priest,
Keep a-pluggin' away.

Delve away beneath the surface,
There is treasure farther down, —
Keep a-pluggin' away.
Let the rain come down in torrents,
Let the threat'ning heavens frown,
Keep a-pluggin' away.
When the clouds have rolled away,
There will come a brighter day
All your labor to repay, —
Keep a-pluggin' away.

There 'll be lots of sneers to swallow.
There'll be lots of pain to bear, —
Keep a-pluggin' away.
If you've got your eye on heaven,
Some bright day you'll wake up there,
Keep a-pluggin' away.
Perseverance still is king;
Time its sure reward will bring;
Work and wait unwearying, —
Keep a-pluggin' away.

CHAPTER 1

Letting Go

Jarvis Buchanan

NEEDS AND AGENDAS

Let us get straight to the point. Letting go of significant people, dreams, or desires is often one of the hardest life skills to master. If you are like most people, you grew up with the intention to achieve your dreams. Those dreams vary from person to person, depending on multiple factors like your family, surroundings, financial stability, and education, to name a few. Maybe your dream is to become a successful entrepreneur or create your own brand and build a legacy. Maybe you saw your favorite athlete or performer making the crowd go wild, which fascinated you so much that you decided to dedicate your life to reach that pedestal, and vowed that one day, you will make it there. Your story may involve becoming that well-respected doctor, lawyer, or engineer you have admired all your life. Or maybe you just want to be and do better than your parents. Well, you need to hear this. No one cares, nearly as much as you do, about your dreams!

I do not say that to be rude, but to be honest. It is the brutal truth; you are, at most, the second character in everyone else's story, and that is okay, because you will realize that you do not care as much about others as you may like to think, either! You may be skeptical of my opinion, but I can prove it.

First, let us see the perspective from a bird's eye view. There are an estimated eight billion people in the world. Each one of us has the desire to accomplish something in life. So, it is safe to say that we all have our agendas. To appreciate this perspective, think about your closest friend, and let us call him Brandon here. Have you ever thought about why Brandon and you are friends? Is it that you simply yearn to be around him? That is potentially the

Live to Never Lose Again

answer as of now, but why did you become friends with Brandon in the first place?

It is important to understand that when we allow any person to occupy time and space in our world, it is because they have a purpose. They meet a certain need. Now the question is, where do our needs come from? Well, without getting too technical at this stage, let us say that we go through several phases of development, and depending on our surroundings, we develop needs. Our culture, families, and environment shape us during our developmental stages, and we derive our perspective from what we see around us. Eventually, our conscious thoughts lead to conscious behaviors. These conscious behaviors become subconscious behaviors, which subsequently become our habits. We derive subconscious habits based on the lens through which we see the world. The habits we form are direct influences of our needs, and it is human nature to have them met. For example, when we are hungry, we eat. If we feel tired, we should rest. So, when you are hungry, food is your need, and your agenda would be to obtain food to satiate your hunger. Likewise, when you are tired, your goal would be to take a break and get some rest.

We all have distinct levels of agendas. An agenda is a plan or general direction you decide upon to meet an objective in life. Usually, we have tunnel vision while pursuing a mission and focus only on completing that. We either live by a methodical plan to achieve that agenda or life bounces us around toward the direction of the energy we put into the world. If your agenda is to wake up in the morning and be upset with the world, then you will find many factors that contribute to your cause. On the other hand, if your agenda is to be happy, you will find a substantial number of people who will support you along this path as well. Unfortunately, agendas are not always that clear-cut,

3

and we tend to judge another person's agenda based on the lens we have developed to see the world.

As an example, take the movie "John Q," in which Denzel Washington played the role of John Quincy Archibald. In the movie, his son, Michael, collapses due to heart failure while playing baseball. Mr. Archibald rushes Michael to a hospital emergency room, where he is advised that Michael's only hope of survival is a heart transplant. Unfortunately, John's insurance does not cover this. Left with no option, the emergency room staff and patients are held hostage by John, until the hospital doctors agree to do the transplant. Here, I would venture to say that when John woke up that morning, he had no intention of holding a hospital hostage, but as his circumstances changed, he found that his means (agenda) justified his end (need). We will get into the right and wrong later but do consider how you would view this situation, or the means John used if it were your son, daughter, mother, or father, who would be in such a dire condition. Your perspective of what John did would change, wouldn't it?

There are two major concerns when it comes to needs and agendas. *First, we establish many needs because of what we experience while growing up. Our culture, environment, and families influence our thinking to a great extent.* This lens is skewed, not because of something we did wrong, but simply put, because you do not know what you do not know while you are in your initial developing stages. In fact, many of our needs are established based on how those around us see the world. Likewise, the lens they were given were, of course, shaped by those who preceded them, and so on. No family or environment will provide you with everything you need. It takes exposure to the world for people to develop their full potential. As a matter of fact, when it comes to needs, sometimes we desire certain unknown or undefined needs, because our environment

Live to Never Lose Again

was so poorly constructed that we manage to replace those missing needs with alternatives to compensate for the gaps.

Second, whether consciously or subconsciously, we tend to consider our agendas over others. Even when we are trying to consider others, we generally regard ourselves first. It can get tricky here.

Let us get back to Brandon and frame his purpose in this book through a fictitious narrative to help you frame your understanding of needs and agendas. You met Brandon for the first time when you were nine years old, a year after your family moved in with relatives for economic support. This move made it the fifth move in the last five years. Along with your family, you were trying to make it work, to somehow sail through the challenging times, but you noticed that even with the relatives' support, it was difficult to make ends meet. Your parents taught you good morals, so you thought that you were a good judge of character. Consequently, you could not be friends with anyone and had no outlet to release your frustration. That was, until you met Brandon.

Brandon was from your new neighborhood. His general impression was that of a spoiled brat, known for getting into trouble and treating people unfairly. Due to his rash behavior, he could rarely be friends with anyone for long. Obviously, this made Brandon lonely. One day, your paths happened to cross. You noticed not only his attitude but also that Brandon's parents were well off, and the family was living much more comfortably than yours. Afterward, you decided to hang out with Brandon so that he would not feel lonely; at least, that is what you told yourself. Over time, his family embraced you. The more you started hanging out with him, the more you got to spend time with his family. Eventually, you began reaping the rewards of being friends with Brandon by getting gifts repeatedly.

Although you projected it as you were being a good friend to Brandon, so as to help him to meet the need of having someone who cared for him, the reality was that Brandon's wealth was providing a sense of value, which was a need you didn't know you had until then. You were subconsciously compensating for your need for validation by masking your intent of friendship with Brandon.

Well, before you start retrospection, please understand that we do not do this purposely; oftentimes, our needs are mysterious. When we have a need, our subconscious will attempt to fill this need through an agenda; in this case, by using Brandon. All you see is that you have a friend that meets a need. So, you put up with his horrible attitude for the feeling of validation you get from being valued and appreciated by his family. You consider it acceptable for this friend to treat you unfairly, and eventually, you justify his behavior and label yourself as being loyal to him, while others are not.

In short, Brandon serves a purpose in your life. Your surface view and what you have come to believe is that Brandon is lonely and needs someone to be his friend. You make yourself believe that you are fulfilling a selfless service by caring for him. But in all actuality, for you, Brandon's purpose is to provide you with a sense of validation besides the obvious benefits. Let us call this situation "the illusion."

The illusion is a concept that can be applied to multiple areas of your life. Start with your family and friends and begin to take note of the needs they provide, and what agenda you choose to accept to sustain that need. There is always a compromise, without which this would not be possible. You are responsible for understanding that compromise and deciding whether it is worth the cost of that person supplying the need. This may get

Live to Never Lose Again

you thinking for a minute, but I challenge you to dig deeper into this theory, because everything you accept comes back to a need.

Why not leave things the way they are? When you are ready to start the journey to never lose again, you must be prepared to be brutally honest with yourself. Before you can let go of anything, you must identify your needs. Otherwise, you do not know what or who to let go of. What is your need? How are these needs being met? Who is meeting them? Are you compensating the person who fulfills the need? Is it really your need, or is it something that you have accepted as your need based on your family, friends, or culture?

It is now time to revisit the statement, "No one cares." The John Q. example as well as the illusion concept, outline our desire to care for others. However, ultimately, we are creatures who have limited capacity to care for the needs of others. Have you ever wondered why people continue to stay in abusive relationships? Many claim that they love their partners and try to justify their abusive nature. They claim to know that their partners are capable of being better; so again, it is about loyalty. However, I would like to challenge that. When you dig deep enough, you will realize that it is a need that the abusive partner is fulfilling, whether it is a fear of being alone, having self-esteem issues, or insecurities, that are masking your need to keep that person as a part of your life. (Side note: If you are in a relationship with an abusive partner, I am not saying it is your fault that they are abusive. I am saying that you have the power to change the situation).

Contrary to what you make yourself believe, the reason for continuing the relationship is not that you, solitarily, care for the well-being of the abusive partner. Rather, it is more about meeting your subconscious needs. You do not care about that person as much as you care about what they provide. That is a hard pill to swallow, but if you want to truly evaluate the situation and evolve into a better person, you must see it for what it is. That is the only way for you to overcome the challenges you face. No one really cares about anyone else's agenda if that person is not meeting your personal agenda, whether you recognize and acknowledge that bitter truth or not. Figure out what needs a person provides and then decide if they deserve that power over your peace.

We all want peace, but many of us are afraid of what we may lose in the process. Throughout our lives, we hide behind masks, scrolling the internet for solutions to surface problems, and shy away from digging deep enough to reach the crux of the issues. This keeps us going round in circles. We attract the same type of people into our lives because we fail to analyze what it is we really need. Trust me, it is difficult to tread on the path of discovering the truth behind the façade, but well worth the trip to hell and back to unlock the secrets of what is holding you back.

When you begin the trip, the pathway is dark, and you will run into so many experiences, circumstances, and memories that force you to run back to the surface. Do not take the easy way out. Just know that every time you turn around and backtrack in fear, you are working against your progress. What is worse, it may prove to be even more difficult to muster the courage to tread on that path again. It is scary because when you give serious thought to the reasons that give rise to your needs, you encounter garbage you may not want to address. You will find that you have unresolved issues with family, traditions, religion, relationships, etc. Keep in mind that, ultimately, no one will care if you decide not to do this demanding work, because the people who are causing you to feel this way have accepted the way things are. They are not reading this book, you are. You are the one with the problem, and you are the only one who can fix it!

Some parts of you may want to accept that as no one person is perfect, you, too, have your flaws, so it is acceptable to deal with those of other people. However, I highly caution you against that frame of thought. One of the most dangerous consequences of not allowing a deep dive is that you leave your fate to someone else. When you dedicate yourself to ensuring that someone else is satisfied, you lose a part of yourself. When you neglect your needs or allow something to compensate for the fulfillment of your fundamental needs, you are vulnerable, and that is because you are allowing an external factor to control you. Let me explain. When you allow Brandon to fulfill the need you have for validation, you have made the need fulfillment external and given him control. At any moment, if Brandon gets upset with you, or if he leaves for any reason, you have a void that you will not be able to fill. Once you reach this phase, you are in a predicament, as you will be willing to cross any boundaries to keep Brandon in your life. You will suffer many types of abuse and wonder to yourself why you should stay in this relationship. You will lie to yourself about why you allow his treatment and do things that you never thought you were capable of to stay in his good graces.

The next problem with external control is that you can never please the likes of Brandon. Once he becomes aware that he has your loyalty, for whatever reason, he will continue to make unreasonable demands until you have nothing left to give. You will wake up one morning and not recognize the person you have turned into, because you have become so dependent on the external factor to fulfill your need. Losing control is dangerous, but do not worry, we will get your power back.

You cannot allow anyone that type of control over your life. *That is why you must do the arduous work of probing deep into your conscience and understanding your needs, and what, how, and who you have chosen to fulfill them.* You must summon the courage to go deeper into the self to understand your needs and what, how, or who you have chosen to fill them. This book is not about becoming happy, it is about identifying the factors that take away your peace and replacing those factors with variables you can control. That is how you defeat the "illusion." Of course, there is an art and science to all theories.

The art of vanquishing the illusion concept requires you to take an inventory of what makes you, you. Often, we are so lost in our worlds that we need help to do this. Do not be afraid to seek counseling if that is what helps you to take account of yourself. This is a part of your freedom from oppression and the most important part of your victory. Keep in mind that you must plan before you start digging. You will need firm determination and immense courage to help you through the process.

IDENTIFYING THE NEED

Years ago, I decided to install a fence around my home. As I prepared for the project, I drew out a plan for the installation. I measured the linear feet and plotted the location of the pickets and posts. After that, I went to Home Depot and ordered the material I needed, and then marked a spot on the calendar for the date I would start working on it. A couple of days before the start date, I reviewed the forecast to confirm that the weather would be favorable to complete the project. That Saturday, I picked up the material and laid out the tools for the job. Everything was going just as planned. I marked the location on the ground from the sketch and started digging for my first post installation. I was barely one foot into the ground, when I ran into gigantic

Live to Never Lose Again

rocks! Unfortunately, the digging tool I rented was not capable of cutting through the rocks. Could I proceed? No. Because I had chosen the wrong tool for the most important job in the entire project — the dig.

In the words of the iconic Mike Tyson, "Everyone has a plan until you get punched in the face." You can have the best plan in the world, but if you do not have the right tools, you will get no further than the surface before you run into rocks that you cannot move with the tools you have invested in to complete the work. Hence, you must be fully prepared for this work. In the case of self-probing, you may choose a therapist as your initial digging tool or resource. Many of us take the aid of our faith to help us pass the boulders. You may need to draw strength from an outside source to begin this process, and there is nothing wrong with doing that. There are times when your own senses do not support you and it is best to take guidance from reliable sources which can help you overcome the dilemma. As a first resort, I advocate for a faith-based source, because it is an internal connection between your higher being and you. However, if you are not religious, I recommend you start out with a counselor, or someone who is trained to manage such situations and is unbiased. At the beginning, you are reinforcing your will to dig deeper, and you may not yet have the tools required to get you past the big rocks beneath the surface.

The initial stage will be tough, as you begin to wage war against the practices you have been following for a long time now. So, let me take another moment to encourage you to find the right tool and continue to dig. Winning the battle is never easy; otherwise, everyone would choose to "Live to Never Lose Again." Just hang in there; your start-up support system will have the tools you need to get you past the first layer. Regardless of

Jarvis Buchanan

how you choose to start, know that a rock is a rock. It is hard, dense, and troublesome to get through. Do not give up or decide to go around it. As you begin contemplation, you will realize that confusion surrounds your thoughts, because you have so many ideas about how you came to be in your current condition. This is a critical point; do not attempt to put the blame on anyone else. *You* must accept that *you* are where *you* are because of the decisions *you* made to meet the needs that *you* have. Playing the blame game never works!

In addition, you must also acknowledge that none of the rocks, which are directly below the surface, are the root of the problem. Examples of surface layer rocks are problems with keeping employment, challenges in relationships, overspending, overeating, etc. These smaller rocks are the illusions that you initially run into but hide much deeper issues. Do not let these obstacles deter you. Do not stop digging for what is really troubling you after you have addressed the direct tensions and try to complete that mission. If you fix the surface problem and stop, you have only bandaged the real issue. You must explore and scrutinize your past mistakes and successes to derive what you need in your life. This is your future, so make the best of your dig and do the work to find the underlying cause of your challenges.

What did I dig up when I went deeper? I discovered insecurity due to favoritism shown to people around me. I discovered a desire to help people, and that I had an excessively kind heart. I had to deal with attachment to people who meant no good to the world or me. I had to contend with religious principles that I could identify with, but to my dismay, were not as dependable as I hoped. I came to the inference that though I had extraordinarily little genuine faith in a power beyond me, I leaned heavily on

Live to Never Lose Again

traditions and words. I realized I was a proud, borderline arrogant person and sought material possessions to give myself a sense of accomplishment. I realized that I am a perfectionist and always want to be the best. I examined each of my surface illusions and asked myself "why", until I found my core needs.

The process helped me to uncover multiple issues, which helped to change me. Having been subjected to favoritism, I subconsciously felt the need for *acceptance*. Behind my excessive kindness hid an ulterior motive to change people into who I wanted them to be. I enabled them to continue destroying themselves and myself, because I could not accept who they were telling me they were all along. I simply refused to believe them, and time and again, I was forced to learn the same lessons repeatedly. Hidden behind my religious principles, I found the need to feel *justified* in my actions. I set unrealistic standards for others as well as myself. My desire for material possessions masked the need to have the *acknowledgment* of others. Underneath the perfectionist, I found a man who needed *validation* from the world.

The common theme throughout, and what I have come to terms with, is that I had never really sat and thought about my needs and the means I had adopted to fulfill each need. Better yet, I have never considered whether I needed the need. You can figure out a lot about yourself by just looking into the past and evaluating it. Are you able to differentiate between filling a need and a need itself? That is why I say, there is no cookie-cutter solution, because your resolution is different from mine and any of the other approximately eight billion people in the world. Take some time and go ahead with your dig without putting it off by giving irrelevant excuses.

Jarvis Buchanan

YOUR ENVIRONMENT

At this point, you have reached your decision point of letting go. It takes analysis as well as trial and error to make decisions on whether you truly have a need for something, or you are simply running according to a habitual pattern and never thought about getting rid of the obsolete programming to update your software to the best version of yourself. Now is the time to start considering whether you are letting go of a need or whether you are letting go of something that is filling a need. In many cases, it may be both. I cannot define a need for anyone. However, I can tell you that you must look at whether you need something, or you have fooled yourself into believing that it is a need due to several years of conditioning by your culture, environment, and/or family.

It is commonly said that if you want to see how a person will turn out to be later in life, look at the mother or father. This connection to one's family complicates matters. Hence, it is not an easy distinction when considering what you need and what you can do without, because we are genetically composed differently based on traits we get from our parents. Of course, you cannot deny that certain characteristics are inherent to you. You have your mother's nose or your dad's pear-shaped head. However, just because we have a genetic code, it does not mean that we are trapped emotionally or socially into becoming someone we do not want to become.

The *China Study*, authored by Dr. T. Collins Campbell and Thomas M. Campbell, advocates that the environmental factors influence who we become as much as our genetic makeup. In this

Live to Never Lose Again

book, the authors indicate, "Genes do not determine disease on their own. Genes function only by being activated or expressed"[1]. An example is given of twins with the same parents and the same genetic makeup, raised in two distinct parts of the world. One child developed diseases that were common to the region he grew up in, and the other child developed diseases common to the area of the world he grew up in. Two children with traits passed from the same father and mother, but with influences from *environmental factors,* produced totally different outcomes. The point here is that genes are your coding, but if the genes are not expressed, they are dormant and have insignificant effect on you.

The doctors make an analogy between the genes and a seed and explain, "It is useful to think of genes as seeds. As any gardener knows, seeds will not grow into plants unless they have nutrient-rich soil, water, and sunshine. Neither will genes be expressed unless they have the proper environment."[2] This research, if you choose to believe, promotes that changing your environment can change which genes you express. Obviously, this comes with caveats and exceptions, such as age, time spent at a location, etc. However, making this revelation within yourself is groundbreaking because you understand that you are no longer limited to believing that you are simply a product of your parents and environment. This also makes you accountable for your actions the day you left your parents. These findings provide you with evidence that you have the ability and freedom to change your environment and surroundings to set the conditions that bring out the best in you.

---

[1] T. Campbell, *The China Study*, (Dallas, TX: Benbella Books), 233.
[2] T. Campbell, *The China Study, 233.*

FINALLY LETTING GO

Arriving at this state of mind allows you to reset your entire system. You can change the need or the source filling the need. You can decide that instead of being dependent on people to take care of your need, you would prefer to internally satisfy your need by opting for any of the extensive ways of expression, be it writing, dancing, art, construction, blogging, or anything that makes you happy; the world is your playground. Personally, I no longer allow pointless conversations that extend past my comfort level to support the habits of people who are not trying to change. *Bottom line is people must want to change to get any positive results.*

So, what did I do? I had these needs for acceptance, affirmation, and acknowledgment from others that lay beneath my surface. These were the needs that I developed during my childhood because of the lens I had developed to see the world. However, through experience, I apprehended that I would never get the affirmation or acknowledgment I needed from another person. After much inner turmoil and trying to grapple with the situation for a while, I understood that the onus lay on me. So, I decided to affirm, acknowledge, accept, and validate myself. Now, it does not mean that I walked through life arrogantly, but it does mean that I gained confidence as I best understood how to treat myself well. The trick to letting go is to understand that science is defining "what" or "who" to let go of, while art is applying the process and executing the release. There were people I had to release, and yes, it hurt to let them go, but with time, that part healed. I executed my release by pursuing my dreams without hesitation and changed my priorities to fit my new appreciation for myself. I also set my clock to surround my needs. No, I did

Live to Never Lose Again

not cut everyone from my life, but I did add my needs back, giving them a priority. I read, wrote, and lost track of time while engaging myself in things I enjoyed. Basically, I began doing the things that supported me to outgrow the old me. I still had something to prove, though it was only to myself. I decided to let go of affirmation from others altogether. I realized that, personally, I do not need to be accepted by anyone. I also realized that I had been sleeping on myself for most of my life, and that my potential was a lot higher than I had ever imagined. Who else could craft the life that I wanted for myself but me?

Did the evolution happen overnight? Absolutely not! It was a work in progress with highs and lows. However, what I discovered was that once I let go of the need to have affirmation and acknowledgment from others, I felt justified in my actions and felt better about myself for making the changes I believed needed to be made.

We will talk more in depth about the process in the forthcoming chapters. Here are the questions to keep in mind as we move forward.

1. Are you ready to let go of something?
2. Are you ready to do the work to let it go?
3. What tools will you use to get started?
4. What needs do you have?
5. Currently, what are those needs filled with?
6. Are you letting go of a masked need or a filler?
7. After you decide what you are letting go of, you need to consider what you are replacing it with.

You may need help to identify the "what" or "who," but I highly recommend you replace the need with something you can do internally. This is the best way to ensure that external changes do not impact your mood, actions, desires, or dreams. After your reflection, the lens through which you see your dreams and goals will change. Your definition of success and goals will change. You will see that you are motivated by your own needs, which are not at all selfish. It is merely taking care of yourself because no one else will care more about you. When you are real with yourself, you will find that you owe only to yourself. When you give life your all, you will attract the type of people who are complemented by what you provide, and you now get to decide if what they provide complements you or not. Not everyone will get this far, as it requires a lot of grit and determination, but if you have been able to, you are off to a great start. You have now put yourself in the driver's seat. What's next?

CHAPTER 2

Validation

Jarvis Buchanan

EXTERNAL VALIDATION

In the previous chapter "Letting Go," you decided that you are done worrying about fixing your situation, and you are ready to let go. We find that letting go is not particularly easy, and that knowing what to release is important, though hard to identify. Thankfully, that work is done, but the journey has just begun. Where do you go from here?

For a start, you must validate the changes you are making. The preceding chapter mentions a few techniques to introduce you to the idea of letting go. However, that is insufficient to give you an in-depth picture, as each person has a diverse set of hurdles to overcome. Therefore, I have dedicated an entire chapter to this, because otherwise, you may end up finding yourself back at the starting point if the appropriate techniques are not present for you to revisit in the harder moments.

[3]Merriam-Webster defines validation, "to recognize, establish, or illustrate the worthiness or legitimacy of" It further defines self-validation as, "The feeling of having recognized, confirmed, or established one's own worthiness or legitimacy."

The distinguishing word that separates the two definitions is "self." Seeking validation from any other source than yourself will destroy your growth. External validation is when a person identifies with the experience of another person and casts a judgment, based on their lens. It is a sign that you approve or disapprove of someone's behaviors and actions. To reciprocate emotions, we allow ourselves to validate or invalidate the actions

---

[3] Merriam Webster's Collegiate Dictionary. 12th ed. Springfield, MA: Merriam-Webster, 2003. Also available at http://merriam-webster.com/.

Live to Never Lose Again

of others. You choose how you feel about someone. Either you agree with someone's actions, you do not agree with their actions, or you just do not care either way.

Take my high school guidance counselor for example. I remember heading to her office one day for a discussion about my future. She and I had spoken multiple times in the hallways, but this was the first formal discussion we were to have about my future. During high school, I maintained a high grade point average. I was more interested in playing basketball and used to indulge in that, more so, as our team was exceptionally good. Until that point, I had not concerned myself with what life had to offer after high school. Like many young adults at that age, I, too, was uncertain, unconcerned, and unaware of what the world had in store for me.

The counselor began to comment on her impression of my grades and then followed up with questions regarding what I thought I would do with my life. She asked me where I saw myself in the next five to seven years. To my dismay, I was lost for a minute, as that is when I realized I had never given it a thought. In short, unfortunately, I did not have a plan. However, I had big dreams, and at that time, I only knew that my plan was to become a doctor of some sort, mainly because I associated it with prestige and money. So, in response to her question, I said confidently, "I want to become an optometrist." She mockingly laughed and replied, "You may need to choose a trade or something a little less challenging."

Of course, I took offense to her response and chose to never consider her for career advice again. However, my mind was now filled with thoughts about my future! In my mind, the challenge was official, and over time, I set off to prove her wrong. After graduation, I decided to make my goal of becoming a doctor a reality. From the 10th grade onwards, I held on to the guidance counselor's words, and made it my business to sign up for medical courses. Well, in my first semester, I dropped the medical courses, failed college algebra and was put on academic probation for my grades.

Not what you expected to hear, was it? What I did not mention earlier was that a huge part of my grades were so good in high school because of the success of our high school basketball team. My high school was rated one of the smallest in the state, but we were ranked as one of the best. During my junior year, we played in a state championship game and lost, but that did not deter us. We doubled our effort and went back and won the next year. The success of the basketball team was a highlight for many in our town. I view it as a wonderful experience, but the problem was that my teachers awarded me grades I did not deserve because of our team's success. So, I graduated with honors, third in my class, and headed to college with unrealistic expectations fueled by the doubt of a high school guidance counselor.

That story ended in temporary defeat for me for several reasons, but the main reason was that I allowed external validation to guide my decision-making. I knew that I had no grasp of basic algebra, geometry, biology, or physics, but my grades reflected that I excelled in each subject. I look back and wonder if the guidance counselor knew that the grades were being passed out to all the student athletes. My approach to continue living under the assumption that I excel without putting in work, eventually caught up with me in college. Her response to my dream did instill a drive in me to prove her wrong. However, the drive was only able to get to the starting point and did not have the fuel to push me past the finish line.

Live to Never Lose Again

There is nothing another person can tell you that will ever be enough for you to get to the finish line. Wonder why? Because there is never a finish line when you are using external victories to fuel your race. Each time you accept a challenge to complete a task because someone told you that you could not, you are allowing an external driver to navigate your course. You may accomplish your task, but because the driver was external, you will not have fulfillment. The reason you do not feel fulfillment in that job, or in that sport, or in that relationship, or in whatever it is, is because you fell in love with the process of proving others wrong. That sort of validation requires you to consistently feed it, and so, you go on with life, accomplishing tasks and receiving accolades and affirmations, but you are never content. You need that constant external motivator to validate your experience. Many people use occupations to serve their purpose.

During my career as an Army officer, I have changed locations and have come across many senior-level officials. As they begin to consider retirement, there is often an unfortunate, constant theme of regret. Incidentally, answering the call of the nation comes with its sacrifices. For many, the decision to dedicate their purpose to the Army is at the stake of the sacrifice of their families, social life, and personal growth. Others have legacies of parents who took the oath of duty due to their sense of obligation. The personal advice I received from the senior professionals was to never allow the job to consume you.

When dedicating yourself to the nation is acknowledged in ways of awards, accolades, and superior evaluations, it keeps one going. But after that phase is over, the soldier or employee is left to ponder whether their decision to dedicate themselves to this cause was truly their purpose. If the initial desire to serve was not through an internal passion for the purpose, then there is a void that no one can fill, because the job will eventually tell you that your services are no longer required. What do you do when you can no longer receive the validation you have come to depend on for so long? Contrarily, if your passion is internally focused, you know that even though you have given your all to an external cause, that job will eventually end, and you take it in your stride. The mindset, which is driving you internally, enables you to transition to support another external source. You can allow your passion to serve as a catalyst to promote any change or growth you want to see happen. On the other hand, if you are tied to anything external, you will have that overwhelming emptiness and no way to fill the void once that external fix is gone. This does not end well for many service members or for anyone in the service for whom the fulfillment of external motivators was the prime point.

SELF-VALIDATION

Without understanding and researching our thoughts, we reduce ourselves to believing what we hear through external sources. Have you ever been around someone who was a die-hard conservative or liberal? Well, in the military, it is not customary to openly discuss your political views. The bottom line is, as soldiers, we serve the civilians who were granted the authority and responsibility of running the country. However, there is always chatter around the water cooler. I do not claim to favor any party, so I tend to sporadically listen to all the Talk Radio stations. Interestingly, if I listen to Fox News on the way to work, later that day, I will usually hear conservative followers using those talking points to validate

Live to Never Lose Again

their positions. On the other hand, if I listen to CNN, I hear the same validation points from liberals too. What is happening here? People are not forming their opinions on matters. On the contrary, we are having our opinions formed for us. This point goes well beyond news broadcasts, but it is a good example of how our experience is often validated by others.

Quite a few people develop a personal definition of self-validation that consists of avoiding the reality of their situation, daily. Self is who you are, and validation is an attempt to accept your concept of who you are. When people come to situations that challenge who they are, or at times, when change is necessary, the validity of self is put to the test. We have an assortment of thoughts that arise when we conflict with ourselves. The challenging times in life require us to take a step back and profoundly refine our definitions of how we have come to be the person we are today. When we are met with challenges like losing a job, being rejected by someone we love, get seriously ill, gaining weight, or any other litany of challenges, it can be devastating to the psyche. It puts us in that vulnerable position of thinking we could achieve something that is beyond our reach.

Many of us cope with our inability to accomplish a goal by encouraging ourselves that we are greater than this situation, or that a particular phase of life is temporary. In later chapters, I will describe the importance of developing your future perspective of self. However, at this juncture, you must accept, with certainty, that manifesting words must be accompanied by manifesting action to synchronize your desire with reality. Any situation *can* be changed if we are able to accept the lesson life is trying to teach. Unfortunately, there is a level of discomfort in changing your norms that you must go through to arrive at your new reality. We all must learn and practice the art of becoming comfortable with being uncomfortable. You must learn to acknowledge that you are not great at everything, and sometimes, we all suffer from setbacks. Whether you like it or not, the opposition is greater than you at some point in life, and that is why you were momentarily defeated. Guess what? That is okay! The purpose of this book is for you to understand how to live to never lose again. To do this, you must process the fact that total loss and momentary failure are two different phenomena. Winners in life use momentary failure to their advantage. Nelson Mandela understood this perfectly, indicating, "*I never lose. I either win or learn.*"

This quote beckons an understanding through the eyes of wisdom. When I reminisce on my "wins" in life, I can smile, because they brought me pleasure and motivated me to want to have that feeling more often. However, whenever I have suffered defeat or bumped my head, I have learned the most about my vulnerabilities and weaknesses. After each failure, we make the decision to classify the moment as a temporary defeat or a total loss. Sometimes, we conclude that a temporary defeat is a total loss and end up giving up the hope that something can be done to change the outcome. The other option is to look at the temporary defeat as a sign by the Creator, showing you how to improve so that you can be strong enough to overcome and win in any situation. Will we be perfect at everything? No. You will suffer defeat from time to time, but we make the choice to either lose or learn from that experience. Once you begin to see that temporary defeat is not a total loss, it is indeed a lesson, and you are well on your way to living to never lose again. *Self-validation comes from looking in the mirror and making the connection between your momentary loss and the lesson life has for you in that loss.*

If you process your ability to never lose again as simply being able to chant a mantra, "I am great, I am powerful, I am a

Live to Never Lose Again

conqueror," you are not practicing self-validation. To grow past your lesson, you must not deny your vulnerabilities by wishing them away. Many folks go through the same challenges over and over because they refuse to acknowledge vulnerabilities, which in turn, is detrimental to their growth. You cannot force self-validation by saying you are validated. You must accompany your mantra with action. This is understanding of the validation process.

You must embrace the emotions by taking risks, trying, and potentially being momentarily defeated. Self-validation is accepting that things do not always work out the way that you want, and learning to exist with the emotions that accompany that momentary failure. Acceptance becomes easier when you embrace the connection between the vulnerabilities and the lesson. Self-validation allows you to cry, scream, be upset, whine, because that may be how you feel in the moment of defeat. Gradually, as you continually trade the emotions of dismay after a loss, for the appreciation for the opportunity to try and learn from each attempt, a strange thing starts happening; you form a habit. You accept that you are not the conqueror today, but you know you have the potential to make it happen one day. You are okay with a valiant attempt and put in a definite effort to change, because you know that in life, both wins and losses work together for your growth. You validate yourself by being yourself and accepting that you may need growth today. Over time, you learn to accept the growth that you can only experience through the process of temporary defeat.

SELF-EVALUATION

Just because you are not doing something substantial today, does not mean that you are stuck in that disposition forever.

However, it is going to take immense effort to become the winner you envision yourself as being. You have some evaluation to do. *You cannot self-validate without self-evaluating.* This means that while you are in the hole you dug to identify your genuine needs, you need to spend some time evaluating what is profoundly important to you. When you evaluate your experiences, you begin to reflect on certain instances or experiences and develop the ability to recognize and categorize your response as expedient or inexpedient. To brief you a bit, I use expedient or inexpedient to describe our emotions about decisions, because if you believe all things work for your growth, then you should be aware that good and bad are relative to time, space, and environment. The decisions we made in our past either navigate us to predetermined locations faster or slower, or we never arrive if the consequences of certain decisions are grave enough.

The good thing about self-evaluation is that hindsight is always 20/20 and you get to clearly identify what you would have said or could have done differently. Self-evaluation is a technique that allows you to look at challenges or failures in your life and connect who you are today with who you want to become. When you look at the trend of your responses to challenges, you see a clearer picture of yourself. It is taking the bird's eye view of your past decision-making matrix and recognizing the trends and consequences that develop from your choices. The goal is to identify the times or experiences where you have momentarily failed and try to find a connection to what is causing the relapse. If a trend exists, this data is valuable in helping to define the type of person you have become today. Self-evaluation is coming to terms with the decision of the person staring back at you in the mirror, and then feeling comfortable with what that person has

Live to Never Lose Again

offered the world to this point in life. Self-evaluation helps you to accept the present moment in life.

Meditation can play a crucial role during the journey to appreciate the person you are today. You must be able to enjoy yourself in the current moment. Even if that person is not your favorite person in the world right now, learn to accept that you are who you are. Perhaps you have made mistakes. So what, we all have made mistakes. Living to never lose again is not about magnifying your flaws; it is about objectively identifying your reactions. The categorization of your decisions also means being honest with yourself and acknowledging that many of your actions were not mistakes at all. Instead, they were reflections of the person you had become. Mistakes usually do not occur continually. So, if it was an accidental action, then you would not have continued to see that trend occurring in your past. If you did the same thing over and over, you cannot call it a mistake; it was your way of living life. In that case, I circle you back to accountability. Do not take the easy way out. Even if you were a low value individual, that is not a problem; no one is here to judge you. However, accept that as a part of your past and avoid labeling those choices as mistakes, because that is a scapegoat that allows you to continue vibrating on that same frequency. The bottom line is that you cannot change anything about the past. Make peace with the fact that what happened, happened. If you have offended someone and if they are still in your life, then make peace with them and move on. It is time to move, and you cannot do that holding on to any of the inexpedient elements that contributed to the old version of yourself.

What do you want to change about your next opportunity to make decisions? The answer to that question is the measuring stick to how you are applying the techniques from this book to your situation. Those answers are your change agents. Those answers are the cornerstones to the foundation for the new person you are building. These new reactions to challenges you face will be the guide to becoming a better version of yourself. Once your foundation is set, you can begin to come out of the digging phase. Be kind to yourself during this time in your life, as it is no easy feat to overhaul yourself.

I can relate this process to weight loss. If you have ever been able to lose weight and keep it off, first, you should acknowledge that the struggle will always be real as long as the supermarkets continue to sell Blue Bell Ice Cream. Second, you know that we are creatures of habit. The habits we form early in life and have subconsciously followed all our lives, are hard to break. We like to think of weight loss as a steady trend in one direction from the starting point, but, honestly, we know that we have our good days, and then we slip backwards. Those who are able to meet their goals understand that their failure is a part of the process. You cannot change years of habits in a day.

So many of our behaviors are automatic reactions that are subconscious to suit the needs of the person we are today. Learning to self-validate takes practice. When you take a bird's eye view, you will *not* see a steady trend of improvement. Rather, you see a volatile, jagged, increase toward improvement. Just like weight loss, you will have days and nights when the new behavior is not yet formed into a habit, and you fall prey to your old ways. There is nothing to worry about. It happens to everyone transitioning from one phase to another. Embrace the imperfection of the process, allow it to happen, but recognize that this is no longer your way of life, and reposition your thoughts. The quicker you

Live to Never Lose Again

can recover from the relapse, the more improvement you have made toward improving your foundation.

How do we do this quantitively? I am glad you asked. To build a more solid foundation, you must set conditions for successfully quantifying your changes and track the results. I am a realist, and realistically speaking, I know it is hard to quantify intangibles, but it is possible. In a 2009 study of the time it takes for form habits conducted by Dr. Phillippa Lally, social psychologist, 96 participants' results indicated that it takes anywhere from eighteen to two hundred fifty four days, with an average of sixty six days to break a habit or create a new one.[4] There is no definite number that works for everyone, but you can set your own goals. To quantify your experiences, consider meditation to evaluate each day. Taking five minutes at the end of your day to evaluate your decisions and setting the stage for the next twenty-four hours, keeps your focus on your goals.

Allow yourself to fail. Yes, you must allow yourself to fail, but manage the expectations of that failure so that you recognize when you are off the new path. This will enable you to quickly get back on the grind without stagnation. The product of self-validation is your ability to "be" the person you are validating. It is less about verbalizing the vision and more about slowly changing into the "I am great, I am powerful, I am a conqueror" person you want to become. It is accepting the ups, downs, and changes that feel weird, because it is so foreign to what you know.

---

[4] Phillippa Lally, "How are habits formed: Modeling habit formation in the real world". *European Journal of Social Psychology* (2009) accessed June 12, 2023, https://onlinelibrary.wiley.com/doi/abs/10.1002/ejsp.674.

You are establishing the new actions as normal. The actions are new to your psychological makeup and are greeted as being abnormal by your current conscious conditioning. You must practice making them normal. Just know that practice alone does not make a man perfect; but perfect practice makes him perfect. Therefore, solely telling yourself that you have changed without doing the work is useless and misleading yourself. The old parable that has survived over two thousand years continues to be true. "Faith without works is dead." Your claim of success must be accompanied by the actions, discipline, and resilience to achieve your goals. This is a day in and day out process of remembering what is important to you and ignoring all other noise. You will get through this! Embrace the suck of the process and get it done. If you are diligent, one day you will notice that you have completed the new task without thinking about it. This is when you know that your mind has accepted the new way of life and no longer rejects the new action as abnormal.

I exceedingly implore you to take effort in finding out what will work for you. This phase must be completed before you can boast of validating your worth and value. Self-reflection and identifying areas where you need improvement and taking action to improve in these areas takes courage. It takes objective review of self, without beating yourself up and suffering through the withdrawal symptoms of the psyche, as the old you recedes, and you are ushered into a new reality. There are days when you will question your judgment, and second guess your new thoughts. This is a normal response because you are entering an unknown part of your life. The body will immediately turn to the fight or flight response. Your initial gut reaction will be to flee from this way of thinking because it takes you out of your comfort zone. This is called cognitive dissonance which is when the mind does

Live to Never Lose Again

not agree with what the body is doing. It is a normal response. You are accustomed to being misused, misunderstood, taken advantage of, ridiculed — all of that. You must develop the coping tools to make getting up every day and enduring the awkwardness of change the new normal. Once you want to change what the mind is accustomed to, there is an anxious response, but accept the response for what it is and allow it to pass.

To bring life to the new you, you must allow the old you to die. The old you is comfortably existing, but the updated version of yourself desires more. The upgraded version knows you deserve more. This is where the actual fight begins. When you are willing to stand up to the conflicting parts of you that are unwilling to change, be firm and tell that part of you, "No more!" No more wasted days, tearful nights, adjusting my schedule for those around me, and being the victim. Be steadfast; you are fighting the toughest opponent you will ever face — yourself.

THE INTERNAL STRUGGLE

This internal fight is akin to the battle of two wolves. In each of us, there are two wolves constantly fighting for survival. One wolf is accustomed to the status quo. This is the wolf that needs external influence to survive, while the other wolf is your true self, and only needs what is inside to survive. The fight for your life is determined by acknowledging that one of the two wolves will always win each situation you find yourself facing. The wolf that wins is the healthiest because that is the wolf you decide to feed.

In chapter one, I mentioned that you have needs that must be met. The needs of the external wolf most likely were being filled first, whereas your internal desires have been all but non-existent. That wolf is strong and becomes stronger every day as you feed it more external satisfaction. So, when you decide to change, you will begin starving that wolf. Have you ever seen a starving animal? It will do anything for its next meal and survival. It will eat itself if it could. Your inner wolf is weak and may need help with fighting off the temptation of giving in to customary satisfactions of the old wolf, because it has been suffering from malnutrition for a long time. However, when you get sick and tired of being sick and tired, you are finally ready for the change. If you a reading this book, you are either there or remarkably close. When this moment comes, your "why" shifts to making you better, and everything else falls by the wayside, and I mean, everything. Although you may be weaker than you have ever been, you are aware that the process of waiting for the starving wolf to lose strength is hard. Nonetheless, you are willing to do whatever it takes to get your power back. When you confront the external wolf, self-validation is born, and external validation begins dying.

It may take you eighteen, sixty-six or even two hundred fifty-four days, but you must commit to the process of owning your validation. At the beginning, you will only have your words and the awkwardness of the feeling when you are making a choice that is not your normal. Your words may have power but must be followed by the actions you choose to apply. Continue to believe in yourself and know that you are beginning the journey. Encourage your growth and embrace that you are not where you need to be, but you now see the greatness of who you are. You are developing into the person you were designed to be without reserve or constraint.

As you change, you will face the tests and have the desire to go back to the "normal." This is where you dig in. You hold on to your belief that you are no longer what or who you were and that you are blossoming to the next level. You are no longer running from your giant but facing it head on. Remember, the external wolf has many ways to trick you into feeding it again. One of the most common is using your environment against you.

What and who surrounds you create habitual thoughts in all of us. One way people try to change is picking up and moving to a new location to start over. If you do this, you are exercising the flight in the fight or flight response. You will eventually fall into the same predicament with a different face and set the same conditions for failure. So, before you change your environment, it is imperative to initiate internal change. That is, identifying your needs, figuring out what to let go of, self-evaluating, and then validating. Once you have completed these four steps, it is safer to consider changing your environment.

Although, as a part of living to never lose again, I promote making changes to your surroundings. If you make changes too early in the process, you will again convince yourself that you have made internal adjustments because of the external changes to the things that surround you. It will not take long for the external wolf to adapt to the new surroundings and get you started on the same path again. But if you confront the wolf first, you have put the deceiver on notice.

The advantage the external wolf has is that it has built strongholds in your mind about people, places, and things that trigger emotions. Those emotions lead you to the same habits. Make no mistake, this wolf will satiate itself, with no regard to your physical or mental health. The hunger is so potent that it can eventually lead to death.

If you remain in the same environment, it makes it much more difficult to defeat the old you, because you are triggered by multiple reminders of the personality you are trying to shed. Some of you may not be able to completely change your surroundings, but you can change the way you commonly do things. Choose another store to go to, read books totally outside your comfort zone, call people you never talk to, or start attending classes for something you have always wanted to learn. If you cannot make any changes to your environment, at least identify your triggers, which thoughts evoke what kind of triggers, and make an attempt to stay away from them. This shocks the system and distracts you from things that remind you of the way you were before. You are making new memories. Each new memory you make takes space from the old memories that triggers certain emotional responses.

Self-validation is all about the process. The time that it can take to change is well worth the positivity it brings for the rest of your life. The challenge is to muster enough courage to face, head on, the things that are bothering you. I am not sure of the type of wolf that is feeding on your life, but you need to know that you are not alone. We all have wolves, and we are all fighting battles daily to keep the external wolf in check. The people on social media who are posting about happiness and wealth are also in this group with us. The few people who can consistently win at life are those who understand the concept of giving up the fear of losing everything that matters to you, because they know that the only thing that really matters is their ability to validate themselves to never lose again.

Here are a few questions to ask yourself:

1. Have you taken the time to self-evaluate?
2. What did you find in your "bird's eye view"?
3. Can you figure out the differences in points where you are being externally validated, and where you are validating yourself?

Live to Never Lose Again

4. Are you willing and ready to take actions to lead to self-validation? If not, then what is it that is holding you back?
5. What can you change in your environment once you have made your decision to change?
6. Can you identify your triggers?
7. Are you willing to let go of the fear and lose it all to gain yourself?

Think over the above questions conscientiously, because that will pave the path for your future so that you do not fall back into being your old self. It is time to set a firm foundation so that when you turn a new leaf and give wings to your dreams, there is no stopping you.

CHAPTER 3

Confront the "L" (Loss or Lesson)

Jarvis Buchanan

GOOD GRIEF

As the journey continues, you are now facing the role of accepting that you are losing something or someone who is important to you. The primary response to loss is grief, which is real and can be difficult to control. It is the body's reaction to remorse. Self-validation will make you feel better, but it does not change the fact that you are human and are bound to have emotional responses. Each day, you will become stronger and learn how to manage the fact that you are pulling yourself further away from the past and into new habits. You can forgive yourself, but it is not healthy to completely forget any event or fail to acknowledge the anguish that comes with your learning experience.

Grief is the natural response to loss, particularly to the loss of someone or something with whom a bond or affection is apparent. We link it to the loss of a person, but we suffer just as much agony when we disconnect from dreams or goals. Let us consider the illusion concept here. It turns out that we have spent an abundance of time and effort on that masked person, who became a part of our daily lives. Despite the changes we are embarking on, the missing link is a void because we are accustomed to the mask.

The weight of carrying a void will probably last more than the habit-building process. I lost my father when I was seventeen years old. My father was a superhero in my life. As children, my siblings, and I grew a deep attachment to our father. He was an older gentleman, and his health began to fail a couple of years before he died. A year or so before his death, I took it upon myself to start having a small conversation with him right before bed. I was drawn to be close to him as his health deteriorated, to capture

Live to Never Lose Again

his wisdom and hold on to the essence and bond we shared. The habit took shape after a while, and I began to look forward to hearing the closing words he always uttered before we ended our chat, which were, "Be careful." A few months before passing away, he became bedridden, but our routine conversations did not stop. Eventually, his health faded until it was finally time to take his last breath. All that was left behind was a longing for more time with him and lingering grief and anguish. After his death, I recall how I continued heading to the room every night for weeks with expectations of hearing those words. It was only after a few weeks my mind was able to process that he was gone, and the habit eventually faded. However, the sorrow lasted for several months. In fact, I still think about him daily, twenty plus years later.

You cannot compare the loss of a loved one to every problem you face. However, the point is, habits will break, but grief is different. There are stages to losing what matters to you in your world. Even if you feel validated by your decision-making, it will take time for you to heal. Oftentimes, we want to stop the mental anguish immediately by moving too fast with something new. I suggest starting new projects or new ideas more apt to your new views. However, you need to take it slow. The void needs to be filled, but you must remember that you are still healing. If you are recently coming off a terrible relationship, it is not wise to immediately fill the void due to your ex's absence by bringing in another person. You need time to focus on yourself. If you have made the decision to stop drinking, it would not be wise to pick up other drugs instead. It would merely mean that you are trading one mask for another.

When you find yourself doing these things, you are allowing another mask to cover who you are becoming. With each loss, there is a lesson to be learned. During the grievance period, you have time to look back at these situations and figure out what positive aspect you can take from it, which is self-evaluation. You must learn to accept grief as a part of the process of growth. The heartache you feel will pass, but the notes you take from that agonizing time can live on forever. Do not force yourself to forget the circumstances but take the lessons from them which boost you for the next phase of life.

ADVERSITY

Lessons are sometimes best learned when there is a deep attachment to someone/something, and you must go through tough times to learn them. Like most kids, my siblings and I were constantly getting into trouble for leaving lights on after we left the room. No matter how many times our parents yelled or complained, we would always need another reminder. It was not until I moved out of my parents' home and into my own apartment that the message resonated. I had recently begun a career in social work, and, at the time, I had little money. When I got my first check, I was barely able to pay my power bill. Trust me, the despair I felt in seeing my check fly out of the window shook me, and from that day until today, not one light stays on in a room after I leave.

It takes tough times to help us have a healthier respect for good times. Think about it. We do not always look forward to rainy days because it inhibits our ability to do things we attribute to our happiness. If it were not for the rainy days, we would take the sunny days for granted. The grievance period is the period the body needs to process the sorrow associated with your void. This time will bring you a greater appreciation of what you have if you allow the process to occur. Healthy grieving allows time to

Live to Never Lose Again

transition your thoughts from what you left behind to what you have in front of you.

This is where people can fall prey to old routines. Unlike the loss of a loved one, when you willingly remove yourself from a situation, you have the ability to willingly move yourself back into that same situation. Agony can become so overwhelming that you think you prefer being in a mask rather than dealing with it. When you decide to change, you will feel miserable on some days, because you miss the experience of the old circumstance.

Just because you are elevating yourself to become the best version of yourself, does not mean that what you were doing did not provide you with happiness, at times. It is imperative to remember your "why" at such times. It is your "why" that helps you bear the grief. The grievance process can go on for weeks or months, but your "why" must be stronger than your "want" at this stage. The "why" you decide to change reflects that although there were times you thought you were happy, you were never truly happy internally, you were never fulfilled, and will never be fulfilled in that space, because it is not a true reflection of who you are becoming.

THE GRIEF PROCESS

The more something means to you, the more grief you will feel when it is taken away. It will take an elevated level of dedication by the new you to get over this period. Sadness itself is not a problem; it is a reaction. Reactions can be changed. However, you must accept that just because you miss something or someone, does not mean that it is, or was, meant for you. We sometimes mix up things that are prescribed as temporary or seasonal, presuming them to become lifetime commitments. Grief will hurt, but there are ways to get around the pain so that you can accept things as they are without recreating more of the same challenges and continuing the cycle.

There are several diagrams of the grief process, and they all lead to the same conclusion — acceptance. Grief will begin as soon as you commit to making substantial changes in your life and begin to cut people or things out of the picture, and, if you want to genuinely live to never lose again, you must be prepared for this step. You have accepted that you are not where you need to be and have also identified what you need to change. It is time to close the deal with your "why" which is worth the cost of your sadness. You can get through the phase with more ease, if you can muster your why in times when you really miss the temporary feeling of happiness, and instead, understand the stages of the process.

In 1969, a Swiss-American psychiatrist named Elizabeth Kübler-Ross wrote in her book "On Death and Dying" that grief could be divided into five stages. Her observations came from years of working with terminally ill individuals. She defines the stage of grief as denial, anger, bargaining, depression, and acceptance. Although not all people experience these steps in the same order, your goal is to get to the last stage without rushing yourself to recovery, because you want the pain to go away. You are in the position for a reason. Changing habits helps to reset your brain, but you must deal with each phase of grief, process the void, and avoid having repressed emotions regarding your situation later in life. These phases will typically begin immediately after you commit to making your initial decision to think for yourself.

Denial: Coping with decisions that you are making to become better can be challenging. Once you decide to initiate the changes,

Live to Never Lose Again

you will question your decisions and **denial** starts the process. Your mind will be brimming with questions like: Is this really happening? Is this a dream? Why did I do that? Is this a mistake? Trust your intuition. It is not a mistake if it aligns with who you know you are destined to become. It is not a dream, and the reality is that it will sting for a while, but it is worth the cost. Remember your "why," and you will be fueled with determination to continue the same path.

If you are drawn off path and experience grief because someone lets you down, know that it is natural for you to become **angry** with yourself, them, and potentially with others. Your train of thought will force you to think in a toxic manner. "I hate them for what they did to me." "I hope they fail." "I hope he gets fired." "I hope I am there to see it when they fail." Realize that in these moments, external controls are still driving you. You are caught up in believing that the external satisfaction of "I told you so" will bring you peace. Nonetheless, what you need to keep reiterating to yourself is that your peace will only come through allowing this stage to pass and remembering your why. It was not to prove someone else wrong, but to prove to yourself that you are able to function and succeed at being a better you. Focus on your journey, because hate for someone else is a burden that you carry for free. Release the anger, and do not hate anyone, more for your sake than theirs. You are becoming better and do not need that hate taking up space during your reset.

Bargaining: This is when you think you can have your cake and eat it too. Maybe I can be the best version of myself, and that person will still play a role in my life, but this time around, it will be with my mask off. Maybe, if I try a little harder, they will appreciate me, maybe if I give a little more, they will come to terms with what they have in front of them, or maybe if I just change this or that, it will change someone else. Time to wake up from your wishful thinking. **Nothing you do will ever change anyone else.** They must change themselves. At this stage, you cannot bargain because the danger of getting caught up again is too costly. The minute you give life to a situation you have defeated; it takes you right back to square one. The work you have done this far deserves to be seen through to the end. Do not bend; remember your "why."

Depression: When depression kicks in, it makes your life miserable and can last for years. It is the long-term effect of developing lasting connections with things we cannot let go of or defeat. If you have lost, you have grieved, and if you have grieved, you have dealt with a type of depression. It may not have lasted long, but you know what it feels like. When you willingly make changes in your life, you will experience depression on some level. In the initial stages of your transition, it is common to have thoughts like, "I am not good enough." "I will always fail." "Why does this keep happening to me?" "What am I doing wrong?"

Get this clear — you are not to be blamed for wanting better for yourself. Your past decisions are responsible for the situations and circumstances you have allowed. Now is the time to be accountable to the new person you are molding yourself into and move on from the situation that tends to pull you back. When you can view your situation from a new perspective, you can accept the decisions that brought you to this point in life. The result of those decisions brought you to a crossroads, and you chose to love yourself, which, at present, is more important than anything else. It results in letting go of whatever stronghold is present in your life, becoming self-aware of who you are right now, and making well-thought decisions as that person.

Live to Never Lose Again

Acceptance: If you allow them, each of these steps eventually lead to acceptance. The grievance period is meant for you to take your time to adjust to the newness of your conditioning. It is not the time for you to reconsider or sway over your decision. If you notice, there is one word that drives each stage of grief and holds your acceptance hostage — fear.

Fear perpetuates each stage of sorrow, and you need either faith from your source and/or assertive actions to get you past each stage. When you lose someone or something and you are in denial, you fear the thought of living without that thing or that person. You do not know the tertiary effects of the loss and how it will affect your life, but you immediately start thinking of ways it will be detrimental to your life. The fear that we associate with denial is the fear of the unknown. You can get over the fear garnished with denial through faith in your source and yourself. If your source is God, you must keep drawing from Him to rejuvenate your mind. I reiterate, meditation requires you to focus on the moment. As denial strikes during parts of the day, use a quick meditation moment to bring you back to the reality that this is happening, and you are still all right.

When you are angry with the world, you have a fear that a person's opinion of you may have been right about who you were all along. You fear that you are what they said you are, and you challenge that perspective with anger and hate. Fear that leads to anger is the emotional reaction to failure. It is a fallacy that you can somehow change an outcome through hate and malice. Anger is a response to the insult you feel when people do not accept you for who you are and what you offer. The anger rescinds only when you realize that you cannot be upset with people for doing what you allow them to do. Do not blame yourself, and do not judge others for their opinions. It is theirs to have, just as yours is your own.

Always keep this phrase in mind. "For every action, there is an equal and opposite reaction." We will talk more in depth about balance later, but you must know that you need to balance out the anger with kindness. Find someone whom you can help. It does not have to be a gigantic deed. Helping others and enjoying minor victories through small, random acts of kindness gives you joy. You need that kindness to balance out the anger and resentment.

You bargain because you are afraid of totally letting go and fear that you have made the wrong decision. The familiarity of the past draws you closer to the temptation of making things work in a way that will benefit meeting the old needs, and you succumb to that. You "what if" yourself to death. This leaves people in a confused state, trying to make sense of how to let go of the past without fully letting go. If you compromise your stance, the circumstance you are fighting against wins, and the reset mode recedes by several notches. This fear can only be defeated through action. Here, you are trying to negotiate the pain away. Use your journal to jot down the pros and cons of the negotiation. Once you start to remind yourself of all the reasons you have come this far, you will objectively see why you need to continue your own path.

Grief feeds on fear and guilt. Although you have taken the necessary steps to change, you still have to face the consequence of dealing with the despair and sadness that follows. You must accept this as a part of the process. The acceptance stage is a safer and more manageable condition. It allows transparency in thought and assists you to derive a particular conclusion about what we label as right or wrong decisions. Instead of viewing our decisions as right or wrong, we can look at them as life lessons or decisions and their consequences. Decisions that work out in your favor today can be detrimental tomorrow. Decisions that do

Live to Never Lose Again

not go your way today are life lessons that can benefit you later in life. By accepting your "L" in loss, you will understand that all things happen for a reason and eventually work out in your favor if you allow them to. These steps allow you to change the "L" you take to have the meaning of a "lesson" instead of a "loss." Be happy that you are capturing the essence of what it means to never lose again.

Questions to consider:

1. Do you accept or reject grief as a part of your growth?
2. If so, can you identify what stage or stages your behavior puts you in?
3. Do you have coping skills to use when you want to turn around?
4. Are you willing to develop coping skills to get you past the grief?
5. What are you afraid will happen or not happen?
6. What is the threat you see because of that fear?
7. Can you release that fear of never losing again?

CHAPTER 4

Your Passion

Jarvis Buchanan

QUID PRO QUO

Who are you now? Well, you made it through the grievance period, and that allowed you to understand the greatest lesson thus far, which is, there are no losses. What do you do with this information? At this stage of life, your perspective about life should be changing. You learn the weight of the anxiety of losing what you fear the most, which consequently drives you to revolt against your core being. Letting go of that fear frees you to become the person who never loses again, but how do you find your purpose in a world you have risen above?

You need to find what you fervently want out of life. The irony of becoming the best version of yourself comes with an understanding that you cannot reach your greatest potential without others. It sounds contradictory, but you need people. Whatever you choose to give to the world must have an audience to receive it. This does not mean you are allowing the audience to validate you. However, finding your passion means dedicating yourself to a cause worthy of your contribution, time, energy, and effort, and people need to see it.

In chapter one, we establish that no one gives anything without an expectation to get something in return to meet their agenda. That basic rule does not change as you evolve; what changes is where the expectation lies. As an example, some parents teach children to share with no expectation of receiving anything back from someone else. The moral that each parent is teaching is that when you identify something that needs your contribution, give it to that person or cause without expectations, because one day, you may be in need yourself.

Live to Never Lose Again

All actions in life are quid pro quo, which means you give something and get something in return. In your mind, you deduce that an action you perform will either help or hurt others, the situations, or ourselves, prior to even executing the action. Sometimes, it takes years to come to that conclusion, while at other times, it is a split-second decision. Daily you are executing actions that will either help or hurt someone or something. You re naturally receiving something from those actions, but it is not always what you expect. It may be physical, mental, or spiritual, but something is returned to you eventually.

Say, for instance, you are trying to get a promotion at work. You have a brief tomorrow that can make or break your shot at a promotion. Your boss, Ted, likes presentations that are meticulous because he is analytical, and you are aware of it. You know your strength is providing the big picture analysis and explaining the slides, but you are expecting that Ted will prefer to see a detailed set of data. So, you stay up all night, preparing a brief filled with numbers, graphs, and bars that explain your points.

Ted, on the other hand, has a longer night than you. His wife and he recently became parents, which has been keeping him occupied. Unfortunately, his wife and child are sick. So, Ted did not get any sleep and feels as if he is coming down with something as well. When you practice your brief, you know that you cannot pull together all the data to make your points clear, but you decide that you will adjust as the brief begins. However, Ted immediately starts his deep dive into your data. You know the data, but you were not ready for Ted's immediate onslaught of questions. He becomes even more irritable because he is aggravated by what he perceives as your lack of mindfulness. What is really happening?

You had this mindset that you would give Ted what he wants, and you were expecting that he would see your ability to provide information in the way he prefers and would recognize how you have gone over and beyond to make this work. Your actions were to produce a certain reaction from Ted. Obviously, you did not anticipate Ted's illness or have any way of knowing that he would be tired and irritable. Your assumption of how Ted would respond is a dice roll, and what you receive in return is the opposite of your intention.

Sometimes you will get the reaction you anticipate from others, and sometimes you will not. The mistake you make in preparation for any activity is that you go in with assumptions of expectations from others. The adage parents teach us about "doing things without expectation" has truth, but it is not the whole truth. You should give without expectation of getting anything in return from others, but you should have expectations from yourself. Without that, you will not be able to move forward in life. In defining your new passion, you should arrange your thoughts around what you expect from yourself.

Let us replay the scenario with Ted. You have a brief that can help you get your next promotion. You know your skill level and what you can deliver. You know that Ted prefers details in his presentation. However, instead of focusing on what Ted wants, you should decide to prepare the brief in the way you are comfortable explaining. That would boost your confidence during the presentation. You deliver the information in a much smoother manner, prepared for the questions that are bound to come your way. You are comfortable with this line of questioning because you presented the data in a manner that clearly magnified your talents.

Live to Never Lose Again

Ted could receive this presentation in a myriad of ways. He is sick and tired, a variable that you did not know until arriving. What you know is that your style of presentation is all that you have to give Ted. Do not have any expectations of how Ted should receive this brief because you know you have given it your best. You gave all you have because your expectation of yourself is to give the best of yourself in any situation.

As you learn the true meaning of being the best you, it is easier to understand that the promotion will come from you being yourself. It is not something that you can force by becoming someone else. Know thyself! If it is meant for you, it will come your way. If it is not for you, you will know by the reaction you receive. Whatever Ted's reaction is, it cannot be categorized as good or bad. It is information, a learning lesson that will guide you to make decisions and plan out strategically for the future. Ted will provide you with the information you need to move forward; whether he approves of your presentation or whether you get the promotion remains to be seen.

Now, ask yourself this question. Where was your focus during the entire analogy between the incident and the hypothetical situation? Was it on Ted or yourself? A promotion will not make people any better or worse at being themselves. You may get more money, gain more power, or more office space, but does it add value to who you are and what you are trying to accomplish? Align the new you in doing things that support your true internal desires, better known as your passion.

WHAT IS YOUR PASSION?

Your passion is hidden underneath all the junk we have piled on top of it. We tend to smother it for the sake of materialistic desires or in hopes of impressing others. It is not always easy to find what you are passionate about, especially since most of us have made ourselves proficient in doing something different during our educational years. From your time in elementary school to our highest level of education, you spend time focusing on what you think someone else wants you to do. Society convinces you that you need a certain amount of money to be happy, and to make that type of money, it suggests various lucrative methods, which may not be in tandem with your passion.

You see your parents struggle through life, or see them successful, and decide whether you want or do not want that for your life. You pattern your life around a career that will make you more like that person to imitate a life that is not your own. However, in all honesty, there just is not a lot of time to think deeply about what you want. People tend to force-feed you what they think is right and their thoughts incline you to think in a certain way. Parents know how hard life is, and guide you away from careers that you are passionate about, so you can become successful as per their lens. They, as well as others, want the best for you, but often, their focus is as blurry as yours once was.

Life's cycles continue. Many parents tell children they need to focus on a difficult stream of science or math, while some parents leave their children to find their own way. Your parents' job is to guide you to the best of their capabilities when you are growing up. Whether you gave in to their choices, or listened to your gut instinct, does not change the fact that you are where you are in life today. There is no magic ball to tell you whether you made the right or wrong choice, about which pill to take when you are young — the red pill or the blue pill. If you take the blue pill and decide to follow your parents' guidance, you may make a lot of money and become financially stable. Alternatively, that

Live to Never Lose Again

career path can lead you to become miserable with what you plan to do with the rest of your life. On the other hand, if you take the red pill and ignore your parents' advice, you may find that the world is not as friendly as you thought, and that money does make a difference. Then again, you may find that you can find happiness, and can make a great living by doing what you always felt passionate about.

The choice to follow your dream, just like the choice to follow another person's will, comes with its own difficulties. However, in the end, we all tend to conclude that we are not at peace when not pursuing what we want to do in life. There is no room for compromise when dealing with alterations of who you are to fit into someone or something you are not.

ANSWERING THE CALL

As an officer in the United States Army, I can say that I get to help people every day. I take pride in knowing that I get to take care of men and women who serve our country, and we all get to defend those who cannot defend themselves. Initially, my drive and passion to succeed drove me to a level of satisfaction in my career. However, there was always a yearning to do and be more.

A few years ago, there was a "so what" moment in my career. Around nine years into my military career, training took me to the military post, Fort Leonard Wood, Missouri. The training was challenging. I recall having days when I dreaded heading to work because it was so out of my comfort zone. Up until that point, I felt the desire to rise to the occasion of the challenge and overcome the situation, but this time, things were different. My wife and I were recently married, and my son was just born. Our living accommodations were around eight hundred square feet of living space.

The challenge, I suspect, began to make me wonder. Why am I doing this? At this point, I had to think back to why I was where I was and decide if and how to move forward. I did enjoy serving, but to be honest, my primary reason for joining was to pay for college. I left myself with few options after I left my community college, without a plan for moving forward in life. When my second year of junior college ended, I went to work at a furniture factory, building sofas and chair arms. The military option boasted to pay for school and gave me a way out of my small town and away from the reckless decision-making habits that I was allowing to seep into my life. So, I took the leap. What did I have to lose, anyway?

My "why" at the time had to do with finding a way to pay off junior college student loans and to attain my bachelor's degree. After countless jobs and almost getting kicked out of junior college, I knew I needed something different and was prepared to do whatever it took to accomplish my goal. The Army offered just the structure and stability I needed. At that time, I was so relieved and thankful for having made the decision to serve because the military did an excellent job of helping me through my lean years. It did so well that I decided to make it a career. However, that drive, like the drive that motivated me to major in optometry, began to fade. I was in my late twenties, when one night, I stood in front of my mirror, and knew that the Army was no longer enough. I am not sure if it was due to the rigor of the training or the birth of my son, but I wanted more out of life. However, but I had no idea what it was. All I knew was that taking care of the soldiers no longer pushed me to want to drive past the challenging days as it once did.

Live to Never Lose Again

What do we do when we want more, but the career is what it is and is not giving us the sense of fulfillment anymore? It provides resources, but it is not what you need. At the training sessions, I struggled daily due to the dwindling passion and an expanding knowledge gap between my peers and myself, which I had no desire to close. Previously, I used to thrive on the fact that I was helping soldiers, which helped me to scratch the itch I have to help people. That worked, but deep down, I knew that the military was not my only calling. In general, I feel comfortable and even invigorated by executing tasks, but it no longer gives me all the fulfillment I need.

I got past that point in my life, using the same techniques I have touted in this book. Nevertheless, it was not an easy task. First, I had to overcome my natural resistance to digging deep and let everything else recede while I reached back to think hard about what I enjoyed doing when I was young. Eventually, I remembered how much I enjoy analytical thought and explaining processes to people in a way that can help them solve life issues. Once I figured this out, it was as if my inner being had been rejuvenated. In my journey, writing became a tool that helped me reach a different audience outside my military circle. With writing, I was able to reach a large audience with a positive message while bouncing around the country serving the flag.

Eventually, in life, people come to terms with reality, whether you took one route or another, the red pill, or the blue pill. If you feel you took the wrong pill or feel like you want to try the other pill, you must figure out how to pull yourself out from the present situation and assess your inner goals without getting too hasty about it. I always want to give knowledge to people in a position of disadvantage instructing that the disadvantage can be an advantage. My passion was hidden under the daily requirements and obligations that I piled on myself. Gradually, as I evolved, I started identifying what I liked and fathomed how to share that new passion with others.

DISCOVERY

It is as important to ascertain your passion as it is to define your needs. Your passion is an intricate part of fulfilling core needs. What you are passionate about will serve as a vehicle for how you perceive success. Once you commit to working in an area that gives you the expectations that you need, you rearrange the priorities of what matters in your life. If you ask someone who has found their passion, when they realized what interested them the most they will generally tell you they have always loved doing activity "x."

Guy Kawasaki, an author, an American marketing specialist, and a Silicon Valley venture capitalist, has explained this concept amazingly well on his website. I would like to quote him here.

"Do I want to make meaning? Meaning is not about money, power, or prestige. It is not even about creating a fun place to work. The meaning of "meaning" comes down to making the world a better place. You can do this in two ways:

First, you can create, enable, or increase something that is good. For example, Macintosh increased people's creativity and productivity. Google and Wikipedia enabled all of us, rich and poor, to access limitless amounts of information.

Second, you can prevent, eliminate, or decrease something that is bad. For example, Tesla is trying to decrease air pollution and our dependence on oil. Palantir and other

Live to Never Lose Again

cybersecurity companies are trying to prevent the bad guys from hacking our computers.

The desire to change the world is a tremendous advantage as you travel down the difficult path ahead, because focusing on a lofty goal is more energizing and attracts more talent than simply making a dollar. And if you do make meaning, one of the natural consequences is that you will also make money.

It has taken me twenty years to come to understand the meaning of meaning. In 1983, when I started in the Macintosh Division of Apple, I wanted to beat IBM and send it back to the typewriter business holding its electric typewriter balls. Then in 1987, I wanted to crush Windows and Microsoft.

I finally figured out that these motivations were silly, if not stupid. Focusing on your competition diverts you from what is really important. The DNA of great organizations contains the desire to make meaning – to make the world better for their customers and for their employees. Having this desire does not guarantee that you will succeed, but if you fail, at least you failed doing something worthwhile.

So, if you are thinking of starting a company, your starting point is to figure out how your product or service will make meaning. Everything flows from the answer to this question."[5]

---

[5] Kawasaki, Guy. "The Meaning of Meaning." March 1st, 2015, accessed 5 May 2023, https://guykawasaki.com/the-meaning-of-meaning/.

Your passion is not about getting accolades. Although they eventually come, because the person dedicatedly works day in and day out towards developing the craft, the deliverable is a payment worth more than material desires. Astoundingly enough, we are working for pay, but not in terms of finances. The pay I am referring to is in the form of attention. We need to be attention from ourselves and from others. Passion needs attention of people to reach its potential. The business of discovering your passion means linking what you were born to do with how you can provide that as a service to help others. This goes back to the "needs and agenda" statement from chapter one. We all have needs and an agenda to meet those needs. Whatever we choose for a profession, it gives us the opportunity to support another person's agenda, because we provide a service they need, and they potentially have something we need (in context with the "quid pro quo" theory mentioned earlier).

To get on someone's agenda, you first need their attention. Ever stopped to think why Fortune 500 companies spend billions of dollars on advertisements? Do you ever wonder why you get so much junk mail? Businesses understand that the more you see their logo, the more you begin to subconsciously associate with them. So, successful businesses focus their attention on how to get and keep your attention. It is the same as Pavlov's dogs and classical conditioning. **Classical conditioning,** also known as **Pavlovian** or **respondent conditioning**, refers to a learning technique in which a biologically strong stimulus (e.g., food) is matched with a previously neutral stimulus (e.g., a bell). It also refers to the learning process that results from this pairing, through which the neutral stimulus comes to elicit a response (e.g., salivation) that is usually similar to

Live to Never Lose Again

the one elicited by the strong stimulus.[6] The more we correlate a business to a demand, the more it becomes a habitual thought of reference to meet a need. McDonald's has mastered it with the "M" in the sky. Anytime your child sees the "M" in the sky, they are immediately hungry, right? Businesses call it branding, and that is the code word for conditioning. They need your attention to the brand or condition you to auto-select their brand over others. Coca-Cola has been around for years, but at the same time, other brands with similar tastes die off. The thirst is there, but your need is already met with the Coca-Cola brand because you are conditioned to think of only that brand when wanting a soft drink with that taste.

People tend to fill needs based on their perceptions of conditions. Your passion surrounds finding a way to market what you have to offer to the people so that you become the best suitor to gain the attention of others. Attention grabbers fill agendas and needs on the condition that they are the best selection. Things get interesting regarding passion from this point. Your passion is not designed to pursue others' attention; rather, it is designed to make others' agendas find you. Remember, you are seeking "attention," not validation. McDonald's does not need your validation, they need your attention, and because they have done so well in conditioning you, their products sell themselves.

This works the same way with people. You do not need anyone's validation either. Others validate whether your offer is for them or not, but that is not for you to worry about. Do not

---

[6] Cherry, Brenda. "What Is Classical Conditioning in Psychology? How It Works, Terms to Know, and Examples.", Theories Behavior Psychology. revised 5 May 2023. accessed 12 June 2023. https://www.verywellmind.com/classical-conditioning-2794859.

waste your time trying to please everyone. Do what is in your heart, do it well, and your tribe will find you. Your goal is to continue in self-validation, confidence, and persistence in making the best product. What is for you is there; you simply need to open your eyes and live free of fear to find it.

Once you identify what you are passionate about, it is time to step up to the challenge of becoming resolute and committed to that task. Now, the hard part is not finding what you are good at but interlinking your passion with the needs of people. How you link to the needs people have, brings you the attention you need and creates a positive exchange cycle where you are producing your greatest work for others who enjoy your work. The cycle loops to support your personal internal expectations of self-fulfillment, and provides others with the external resources they need to refill themselves.

In each connection we make with people, we become a part of their quid pro quo cycle. We interlink ourselves with their needs and agendas, and likewise, they become a part of ours. The stock market is a good example of the process of how passion feeds agendas, and how agendas feed passion. Portions of the stock market called "futures" are considered zero-sum games. These contracts represent agreements between two parties, and if one person loses, then the wealth is transferred to the other. This means one person's *gain* is equivalent to another's *loss*, so the net change in wealth or benefit is *zero*.[7] With passion and

---

[7] Kenton, Will. "Zero-Sum Game Definition in Finance, With Example." Futures and Commodities Trading Strategy and Education. Revised 16 August 2022. Accessed 12 February 2023. https://www.investopedia.com/terms/z/zerosumgame. asp#:~:text=In%20financial%20markets%2C%20futures%20and%20options%20 are%20considered,then%20the%20wealth%20is%20transferred%20to%20 another%20investor.

Live to Never Lose Again

agendas, there is not more passion than there are agendas that need to be filled, and no more agendas than passion to provide for that agenda. If a new passion is discovered, there will be an agenda that needs it, or the passion will die. Similarly, if there is an agenda, and no passion to fill it, the agenda will die. You can also equate this to supply and demand. If there is a demand and no supply, a demand dies, and if there is supply and no demand, the business dies.

Once you identify what that passion is, it is time to relay it to the world around you. Your passion allows you to give your best effort in what you are naturally good at doing. Each of us have an innate sense of doing something better than others, either because we were born with it or picked it up along the way. The cost of spending your attention on developing your passion will be worth the payment of the attention you will receive once you have mastered your craft. Grabbing the attention of others allows you access to the needs, agenda loop, but how you use the attention dictates whether you are using your passion in the right way.

IDENTIFYING YOUR PASSION

There are no losses when you are pursuing what you love to do. There may be temporary defeats because you have not figured out how to become a part of the passion agenda cycle, but there is no permanent failure in pursuing your interest, because it satisfies you internally. You are good at it and do not have to change who you are to get it done. The business of leading a team in a field you are passionate about makes you unstoppable. We need to ensure that our focus is on our field of interest and not on a label. Many people answer the "what am I passionate about" question wrongly as they first look at the label's life offers. We ask ourselves or to our children, "What do you want to be?" and then proceed to use the laundry list of prescribed occupations to force who we are into that box. We say things like, I like doctors, and I met a cool one at one point. We think I want to be an architect like my dad, or play sports like my mom, without taking time to consider who we are and our own purpose.

We force our passion into a box by making ourselves victims of the roles of modern society. If you understand your passion area and are aware of who you are in life, you know the ideal person you want to become. On a specific occasion, while speaking at a University, Denzel Washington told the crowd of students to "hang in there." That statement is short and concise but carries much weight. He went on to narrate the beginning of his career and the pitfalls he faced. He mentioned how he would have essentially taken anything in the realm of acting or entertaining to exploit the talents God had given him. However,, he did not box himself into becoming an actor, and tried singing, dancing, and a host of other things within range of his passion area before he found what catapulted him to his personal success. His passion area was to bring joy to people's lives through a form of creative art. It is difficult to fail when you become well versed in a passion area and your "why" is shaped broadly to fit a broad genre. Being open to what life presents and molding it with your will and vision is the distinction between achieving for the sake of a label and becoming your best version of yourself for the sake of self-fulfillment.

We all have talents unique to us. However, we fail to answer the factual questions regarding our passion — why. Why you want to become a doctor is more deep-rooted than the aforementioned reasons. Simply put, if you are passionate about something because

Live to Never Lose Again

of someone else, it is not your passion. If you can honestly answer the question of what your passion is, you will find that the answers are less defined by labels or today's professions. Truthful answers sound more like: I like to help people; I like to see people smile; I like to fix things; I like to organize; I like to protect others. Notice that all these are services where you can use your talents to shape you into becoming an exemplary. There are many ways to accomplish your ideal purpose. If you start doing that thing religiously, you stop fearing the thoughts of others and fall in love with the process of becoming what you are meant to become.

In the Bible, there is a parable about talents. Talents in that context was how money was defined at that time. A rich man went out of town. Before he left, he gave talent to three of his apprentices. He gave five talents to one, three talents to another, and one talent to the third man. The man who had five, went out and earned five more. The one with three did the same. However, the one with one talent buried his talent to ensure its safety. The rich man returned and asked the men to report on what they did with their talents. The man with five talents reported that he used his five talents and bought back an additional three talents. The man with three talents indicated he used his three talents to bring back three additional talents too. The man with one talent relayed he buried his talent to ensure it was safe while the rich man was away. So, the rich man, in all his wisdom, took the one talent from him and gave it to the man he had given five talents.

The law of use requires us to utilize our talents, both money and skill. This is why the rich get richer and the poor get poorer, or you hear the saying, "Scared money doesn't make money." If you have talents, you *must* use them. These talents are your blessing and will make it much easier for you to find success in your chosen field if you find a way to align them with the needs of people. Do not push yourself to become something you know will not make you happy. Instead, focus your attention on answering the root question and plan from that point forward. This process will save you time and bring you peace.

You will be successful and find your peace if you stick with it. Those who can preserve are lucky enough to make it to the relationship, where work is play. The good news is that many will give up, so there is room for you to carve your path. Prices Law is an indicator of what you are up against in terms of competition in you field. This law is a depiction of business predictions, but many have found it relates well to life. The law simply states that 50% of the work in a general field is accomplished by the square root of the total number of employees. This means that if you have twenty-five people who are doing work in an area, then five of them will bring in 50% of the sales or rewards.[8] Those are the ones who stick with it. Those are the people who do not quit and are dedicated to their passion. I challenge you to become the 5%.

There are a few questions I find helpful in discovering your passion.

1. First, think about what it is that you would do for free. If no one paid you any money, what is something that you would do for no money at all? What is something that you do, regardless of any form of payment or attention? What is something that you are drawn to do naturally?
2. When you wake up on a Saturday morning, or any morning when you do not go to work, what are the

---

[8] McCallister, Nate. "Price's Law – What It Is and How to Leverage It to Change Your Business." Entreresource. 21 June 2021. Accessed 14 May 2022. https://entreresource.com/prices-law/.

Live to Never Lose Again

things you naturally yearn to get done after your routine tasks are complete?

3. What things have you naturally done, from childhood till now? You may not have done this task daily, or even weekly, but it has stuck around all your life.
4. What do you do, whether times are good or bad in your life? What is your fall back? Do you have something that you do to bring you back to reality when you are hit with shocking news? What makes you settle in and come off the high or the low?

Lastly, what do you read, talk, watch, or teach others? Often, this is a sign of what we are passionate about, contributing our efforts towards it. Your passion will not be the next big thing you see on TV. It will be something that has been inside you since you were a child. Once you are in it, you will know.

In the words of LA Reid, "Find your passion, and it's no longer work." When you are passionate about your work, you will have that confidence in your voice and a spring in your step. What could be more fulfilling than this? Hence, identifying your passion will help you to map your future.

CHAPTER 5

Life Cycles

BEHIND THE SCENES

If you notice people in their work environment, it is easy to tell when someone is enthusiastic about their work. Our identity lives deep within each of us. Finding your identity is challenging because there are more facets to you than you may think, and multiple contributing factors which help to shape your view of self. Most of what we have discussed thus far has dealt with identification. However, another factor of life that must be examined through your new awareness lens is life cycles.

Life cycles are recognized only when a person reaches a level of wisdom that allows them to remove themselves from the direct cause-and-effect relationship to see a broader, more dynamic design of life occurring. Life continues to happen. We cannot take timeouts or dictate when we need a break. When you can define yourself and the life cycle, you become an expert in the 'live to never lose again' mind frame. This type of recognition takes time to understand and distinguish, but when you reach the point of identification, life becomes much easier.

When I think about the "easy life," I consider two age groups. Childhood, which is prior to adolescence, is generally an easier time. The resilience of children to overcome insurmountable odds and to maintain hope where only the dimmest light flickers through, is because, at this age, life has not yet shown its power. Life is easier, children heal easier, believe easier, trust easier, etc. Notice, I use the word "easier" and not "happier." Children have tools that make life easier, but that does not always equate to happiness. I do not promote that life treats all children the same in terms of their parents' social or financial status, but children have an innocent, invincible imagination that is coupled with a

Live to Never Lose Again

short-term memory. This allows them to shelter themselves in their imaginations and tuck away reality, leading to a fantasy life. However, as we know, those repressed memories do come back to visit us once our imagination fades and reality settles.

It is not until years later that we reach the second group who live the easiest, but again, not the happiest life. Senior citizens have been through everything life has had to throw at them, seen some of the best and worst, and are still here. I am not referring to sixty or sixty-five, but more around eighty to ninety-year-old matriarchs and patriarchs. Whereas children do not know how life works, senior citizens reach a point of just not caring about life's antics. This mindset is platinum status to live to never lose again. They allow life to do what it does and adjust how and when they can enjoy one moment at a time. During a horrific storm, with tornadic activity brewing around us, I remember asking my grandmother, who was well into her eighties at the time, "Mama Rene, what are you going to do if lightning strikes the house?" Her response at the time did not resonate as much as it does now. She replied with a question of her own, "What can I do?" She did not worry about storms she had no control over.

I have used the term "storms of life" a few times. As you have assumed, a storm in life is a time when you consider yourself facing a tragedy or crisis. When you have lived through enough storms of life, you understand that the game of life is about cycles and frequencies. Hang in there with me; again, I promise not to get too philosophical, as this is a practical approach book.

The live to never lose again attitude is rooted in awareness. Obtaining a state of consciousness that recognizes the zeros and ones behind the coding establishes the connection that contributes to shaping individual thoughts, aims, and actions. What I am saying is, everything you are going through has an obvious cause-and-effect reaction, but awareness is hidden behind the scenes. The human body is an example of cause-and-effect complexities hidden beneath the surface. Take a moment to clench your fist and then release the tension. Squeeze and release are simple actions. However, the live to never lose again attitude considers the actions behind the action. What actually happens when you squeeze your fist? a neuron or nerve cell transmits a signal through the body. A part of the transmission process involves an electrical impulse called an action potential. This process, which occurs during the firing of neurons, allows a nerve cell to transmit an electrical signal down the axon (a portion of the neuron that carries nerve impulses away from the cell body) toward other cells. This sends a message to the muscles to provoke the response to clench your fist. [9]

So, on the surface, you see a hand opening and closing, but there is a series of communication cycles firing to produce an elicited response. We did not have to teach our neurons to fire, so we tend to not spend time pondering over how it all works. On the other hand, we do control the thought that provokes the response and the action itself.

I will bring this point home with a more literal example. Imagine a six-year-old child who is acting out in school. Every day, the child goes to school and wreaks havoc in the classroom. He hits other students, talks excessively to the point of disturbing others, and often finds himself in the principal's office. Using the example from above, the child's actions are the surface-level responses that we often desire to control. On many occasions, we

---

[9] Cherry, Kendra. "Action Potential and How Neurons Fire." Theories Biological Psychology. Revised 19 November 2021. Accessed 15 October 2022. https://www.verywellmind.com/what-is-an-action-potential-2794811

Live to Never Lose Again

label the child as "bad." We look to solve the immediate problem by medicating the child to control the acts of violent behavior and his inability to concentrate. We simply do not have the time, understanding, or empathy to look beyond these behaviors. The few who are willing to accept that the child's actions are not directly related to what they see at school and are diligent enough to probe, always find that the misbehavior at school is not a result of an ill-mannered and spoiled child wanting to do mean things. The neurons firing in this child's life are linked to issues like parents who are on the verge of getting divorced, an abusive parent, a father who beats his wife, a mother who beats the child, a brother who uses drugs, an absence of love and nurture, a hungry stomach, or lack of attention. Any or all these actions or neurons firing are the reason for the impudent behavior of the child at school.

Why is this important to understand? Your ability to empathize with the condition of the individual alters your reaction to the behaviors they exhibit. When you consider the neurons that elicit the response, you do not take things personally. Essentially, you change your thought process about the person or situation. This is pivotal in turning any negative aspect into a positive one. We discussed the internal dig in the previous chapters. Finding out what is inside is merely one-third of the battle, while learning how to decipher the coding in the external world has its equal portion. Finally, the skill to make the two work together completes the equation.

What's Inside (the dig) + Internal Coding (behind the behavior) = Live to Never Lose Again Mindset

For this equation to work, we know that change must happen at the neuron level. As indicated, neurons are facilitators of thought. A neuron is a neuron, nothing more, nothing less.

It is charged by an action potential that helps turn our thoughts into actions. Let us use another example for better clarity. We cannot change the attributes of a wire, just as we cannot change a neuron's response. However, what we can change are the thoughts we think and the response it elicits. Picture the wiring behind the walls in your home. We walk in, flip a switch, and a light comes on or a fan starts to cycle. Here, what happens is that the intricacy of wiring receives an electrical charge from a power distribution box that carries a current to the fixture of your choice. A switch is flipped (stimulus), and a fan or light comes on (response). This exchange is like your thought pattern, as a person thinks, and the neurons respond to execute that action. Now that we are keeping a tab on ourselves, it is time to realize that to evolve, thoughts must change, and it is time to investigate how to change those thoughts.

Your level of awareness and how you perceive everything that happens in your life determines if you are prepared to receive the lesson life is attempting to teach through failure, or if you will continue to become victim to the same trigger response. The connection to understanding life cycles and living to never lose again is understanding that individual development relies on your ability to relate and allow. We often take situations and shape them into what fits easiest into what we know or how we think life should be or become, instead of allowing life to be what it is, and appreciating the experience of learning. The quicker you can learn to see through the walls of the storm, the sooner you never lose again. Your x-ray vision is in direct correlation to your ability to relate to another's experience.

However, this does not necessarily help your immediate grief. There will be times when your decision-making cycle will not support this frame of thought. If you ever want to come out

Live to Never Lose Again

of that storm completely, then relate and release. When you do that, you allow and accept the situation, which propels you to rise above the storm, and this is where your peace is hiding. This is where you can never lose again. You must have now understood the process of surviving the storm, which is, to recognize the storm, review what lurks behind the walls, relate, and appreciate the existence of whatever that is or was as a lesson. Lastly, you get to choose.

In every situation in life, you have a choice. This is important to understand. You are never trapped! You can choose to:

a. Change nothing.
b. Change the situation.
c. Change yourself.

Each of these choices will help your growth. However, all decisions are not expedient. Welcome to the game of life. You are a player, and life will not stop until your last breath. However, life happenings can be neutralized or at least contained. Just remember this — life always gets a vote when we are making decisions, and that vote is rarely cut and dry. It takes your x-ray vision to understand the lesson. Otherwise, you will learn that same lesson over and over for the rest of your life.

CATEGORIES

Sometimes, life works in not-so-clear terms. There are storms that life creates as lessons that we need to learn. Sometimes, it takes us years to learn these lessons, but the formula remains the same. Those of us who can live to never lose again, remember the answer from our last storm and use that knowledge as a lesson for the next one. We recognize that the process of solving the equation does not change and always ends up with the same options — leave things as they are, change the situation, or change ourselves.

Some of you may believe that changing yourself is the answer. There is nothing wrong with growing as a person. In fact, I promote change as a healthy way of adapting to the storms of life. To help you navigate the route that will lead you to productive change, I will explain the categories people fit into, from my lens. There are multiple ways and means for helping you define who you are, ranging from personality to identity tests. While these tests are valuable, I revert to simple explanations of what my eyes can see from natural phenomena that occur in day-to-day life. The simplest form of describing people through my lens is that we tend to migrate to one of the three categories: dwellers, achievers, or dreamers. It tends to be who we genetically start out as and who we return to, regardless of how far we may move from that point of origin.

Dwellers:
The dwellers' point of origin is comfort. They work hard to sustain a comfortable way of life. Dwellers prefer familiar surroundings. They will work hard or hardly work at all, as long as the means bring them to the end state of comfort. These are the "relaxed" ones in life. The upside to a dweller is that it is difficult to take away their peace because they do not chase dreams. The downside is that they sometimes wonder "what if." Dwellers work well in organizations that provide security, balance, and order.

Achievers:
The achievers' point of origin is external success. They chase external accolades. The challenge of attaining Fortune 500 success, being on the Wall Street billionaire list, or being honored

Live to Never Lose Again

as the "CEO of the Year" drives their performance. These types of people are extremely competitive and thrive in situations that allow them to challenge themselves against structural guidelines and metric monitoring systems. These people are compelled to take on tougher projects and feel out of place in areas that require them to relax for too long. Generally, achievers work best in industries that require a high operational tempo.

Dreamers:
A dreamers' point of origin is internal success. They chase internal approval for themselves. These people are typically the artists, dancers, and free spirits of the world. They challenge social constructs. Being passion chasers, they are typically blind to accolades and are unable to relax unless they are working towards what they see as their passion. They can make great entrepreneurs but tend to skip the steps of defining their passions. So, they chase multiple areas and may find some success but never feel satisfied. However, they are on the other end of the spectrum; they never wonder "what if" because they constantly take risks or start projects.

Dwellers, achievers, and dreamers all work within the confines of their character types. Look at your past few jobs. Were you happy? Now, use the definitions above and ask this question to yourself — Were you in the right place, according to the type of person you are? That is important to understand when considering a change. If you did not do well at a position, do not be so hard on yourself. It is quite possible that the job was fighting who you were as a person.

You can also use this technique for evaluating the people in your circle. Are you constantly wondering why some people never "get you?" Do you wonder why people cannot follow the simple plan you followed to get where you are? It could be that they are not built that way. To the contrary, if you see people at peace, and wonder why you are always rushed and never in control, which may be because you are not built that way.

No category is better or worse than another. We must acknowledge the categories co-exist in harmony, and appreciate each person for who they are, and not who we want them to become. It is also about knowing who you are and which category you belong to, so that you are not upset when comparing yourself to others and not seeing that same level of success. The universe is constructed on balance, and that balance permeates into all things. There are just enough dwellers, achievers, and dreamers in the world to maintain the rotational balance between the types of people, needs and wants, supply and demand, etc.

STORMS OF LIFE

Next is understanding how the categories work in conjunction with the storms of life. In his book "Life is in the Transitions: Mastering Change at Any Age," Bruce Feiler indicates that life does not happen in a predictable linear pattern. He defines a disruptor as an event or experience that interrupts the flow of one's everyday life and states that they are distributed across life, happening whenever. Disruptors are deviations in a person's life, and he estimates that one in ten disruptors become "life quakes," which are forceful bursts of change in one's life that eventually led to renewal. He calculated that the average of such situations for any individual is three to five times in a lifetime. Further calculations indicate that 43% of life quakes are voluntary, which means, we initiate the change ourselves, while 54% were

Live to Never Lose Again

involuntary, which means, things that occur outside our control. [10] (Chapter 3)

I prefer describing life quakes as the storms of life or cyclones. Over the course of the next few pages, we will go through a generic example to help describe the cycles of life and how cyclones are better suited to help you make the connection. In life, there are fixed variables, for instance, our genes or DNA. Genes are under the category of things we cannot change. They are constraints we must identify and learn to work around.

To understand this concept, we will follow Jason, a young man, who wants to be a professional basketball player. Jason was born with the genes to become a well-bred basketball player. Both his parents played college basketball and were tall. Inherently, he was always taller than everyone around him, which was a bonus in the game. All through his youth, he could be seen with a basketball in his hand. Jason's parents had to drop out of college midway through, because his mom had been pregnant with him, and they could not afford to stay in school. Therefore, Jason's environment was considered lower class.

By default, we are given genes we cannot change and an environment we must adjust to thrive in. With these variables in place, we envision routes we want to take in our lives to reach specific destinations. The plan becomes an idea. The word idea, which is a thought, notion, or concept, is important to remember. Ideas give us a path to navigate but are susceptible to life's cycles. Life cycles are a series of life events that repeat in the same order, similar to cyclones.

---

[10] Bruce Feiler, *"Life is in the Transitions: Mastering Change at Any Age."* (London, England, Penguin Press, 2020), Retrieved 15 January 2022. from https://www.audible.com.

A cyclone is a large-scale air mass that rotates around a strong center of low atmospheric pressure. You may be more familiar with the term hurricane, which is synonymous. The calm eye of the storm plays a part in maintaining a storm's force. Each cyclone has three major sections: rain winds, the eye, and the eyewall. The eyewall is significant in understanding how the storms of life cycle through our realities. As described by geoscience data, the winds and rain can extend up to hundreds of miles from the center. The thunderstorms which spiral slowly counterclockwise, give strength to the right side of the cyclone, which is relative to the direction it is traveling in. In addition, the east side or right-side winds increase the storm's surge.

The eyewall of the storm is the dense wall of the thunderstorm surrounding the eye and has the strongest winds. Then again, the eye is calmest and clearest. People in a hurricane are often amazed at how the incredibly fierce winds and rains can suddenly stop and the sky clears when the eye is directly over them. Then, just as quickly, the winds and rain begin again, but on the opposite side.

Sometimes, when we are linked to an idea and have honed that idea to a specific label, such as a type of doctor, lawyer, professional basketball player, or football player, we focus our attention solely on this one goal. We work hard towards this goal and do everything right to achieve it. However, we forget that life gets a vote on whether you achieve that specific goal or not. Out of nowhere, a cyclone arrives. Cyclones take many forms, such as an accident, a health crisis, or a loss in the family. Cyclones leave you with three decisions; stay the same, change the conditions, or change yourself (recognize the theme?). The key point is, if you recognize that no matter where you are in life, you will always have these three choices, you are *never* trapped! The only choice

Live to Never Lose Again

you do not have is whether to weather the storm, as it has either already arrived or is around the corner.

Here we pick up again with Jason. Time passes, and he continues to practice and grows a lot as an athlete. He went on to become the best player in his neighborhood, then junior high, high school, region, and so on. He is a highly sought-after player and decides to attend college. After having a successful first year along with his teammates, he decides to celebrate it. On the way back from the fraternity party, the driver falls asleep. Jason is severely injured but is alive. Unfortunately, he loses the use of his legs.

For Jason, if he chooses to stay the same it essentially means he continues to dwell on the situation with no effort to overcome it. He knows well that without the use of his legs, professional basketball is out of the question, but he has stopped looking at things pragmatically. The storm's wind and rain will continue to abuse him because he refuses to move on. This can lead to depression or worse. A second option is for him to completely overhaul his desire and change the blueprint from scratch. This option can be like the roll of dice, and you may find yourself bouncing from job to job until you can find something that allows you to feel fulfilled. The last option is for Jason to change his conditions and move on with his goal but from a different angle. This option requires Jason to try to navigate through the storm and remain in his passion area.

Many people believe that your passion is associated with a particular job — doctor, lawyer, professional player, soldier, to name a few. Remember from the previous chapter, passions are less specific and offer you the chance to work within an area. Passion areas create flexibility and offer multiple modes to get you to your goal. After considering multiple options, when Jason gives it serious thought, he decides to choose the modified route and continues to work within his passion area of basketball. This option gives him hope that he can still achieve a goal. This is critical. He needs to have hope that he is working toward success, or he will lack the fuel to get through his crisis. However, without the use of his legs, realistically, Jason knows he will never become a professional basketball player. To begin the transition, he must do two things. First, let go of an idea or goal that he has conditioned himself to want more than anything else, and second, allow himself to go back to his beginnings and choose another idea, which is within his passion area such that it aligns him with the common activities that bring him joy.

A life storm can be managed and weathered better by understanding why it came into your life. No calamity comes to simply cause you pain, whether it is voluntary or involuntary. For Jason, the storm hit, toppling all his plans for his future, which is why the decision to change his idea will be difficult. The accident and letting go of the original idea is the right side of his life storm. The winds will blow strong because we are conditioned and have worked hard to develop habits that support our goals. We tend to hold on and dwell on our past, often wondering what would have been instead of what is. Once Jason accepts that he must move on from a specific idea and is able to let go of it, he is past the first part of the storm and ready to move on to the next, the eye.

The eye is when you find peace in allowing the previous goal to slip away. You allow the grievance process to take its own time, but eventually, the habits subside, and you allow the newness to settle in. You feel better, but you must be careful during this time, because there is indeed a third side, the left side of the cyclone. This side symbolizes growth and more acceptance. You must now

Live to Never Lose Again

develop a new skill and modify the blueprint to recondition and develop new habits. It is theoretically ideal to move forward, but it is not easy to replace your idea, which you may have nurtured for a long time, with another idea. At first, you will feel like you are forcing yourself to love something that you do not love. However, if you take the time to go back to your roots, you will know that is not true. It is simply the awkwardness that exists in the mind, accepting unfamiliar behaviors in unfamiliar territory. Stick to it. You will learn to love the new idea because it is still within your passion area. For Jason, he decided if he could not play, he would coach. By choosing to become a coach, Jason still gets to be around the sport he loves, contributing to the lives of others while continuing to challenge himself to strategize, compete, and win at the game of basketball and life. We must learn to accept situations like Jason did. Every cyclone in our life is a great opportunity to grow if we understand our choices and are willing to accept that life gets a vote.

Questions to ask yourself:

1. Are you a dweller, achiever, or dreamer?
2. Are you in a storm?
3. If so, how did you get there? If not, look back and identify your last storm to help develop a better understanding of self.
4. What will you do if you are in a storm? Keep things the same, change the condition, or change the blueprint?
5. What are other options if you choose to change the condition or the blueprint?
6. Are you willing to try one of these innovative ideas?

CHAPTER 6

The Intangibles

FOCUS

The business of accepting a new idea is about becoming aware of "who" you are, and putting "what" you are, or the conditions that made you what you are, in alignment. All roadblocks in our life have intended effects. Your perspective regarding these effects determines how you overcome them. One option is to simply accept it as life happening, and the other is to understand the purpose and grow in that direction. Jason was at the red pill or blue pill decision point; either accept the storm as life raining on him or learn to grow from the mishap and use it as strength. We know he used his experience to grow, which meant letting go and rebuilding. He has chosen the route of changing the blueprint to achieve a slightly different dream. To make this new dream a reality, he needs to focus.

Focus while bracing for a storm is akin to the sugar that makes the bitter medicine a tad bit acceptable. It is taking the unpleasant situation and making it pleasant by introducing a positive idea that can dilute the negativity. Focusing on this new, positive idea is pivotal in your transition. Focus is the center of activity or interest. It is not enough for Jason to become aware of what is happening. He must also envision himself as being who he wants to become. This vision or imagination is the sugar! The more vivid and clear he paints the picture, the sweeter the potency of the sugar.

How does Jason focus on the sugar? It is possible to do so through habitual thought. The first step is for Jason to train his mind to focus on the vision of the best version of himself instead of the current version of himself. The next step is for him to let go of the fear of not becoming a basketball player and instead

Live to Never Lose Again

focus on the faith of becoming a terrific coach. Although you have thousands of thoughts a day, your mind can only focus on one thought at a time. *Your faithful thoughts must outbalance your fearful thoughts.*

With practice, faith in what you will become will present itself at the forefront of your mind. Constant thoughts will become actions as you continue to build habits of the positive mind frame. "Embrace the suck" as we say in the military. Embrace the negativity and change the narrative of your life. To do this, change negativity to positivity by changing the conditioning of your thought patterns. You create a new you and have one focused thought at a time. When you can do this, you get the message that you never lose, and that every obstacle has the potential to benefit you, but that is only if you are ready to accept the change and appreciate what life has to offer.

Now is the time to focus on yourself. When your focus is on achieving a label for the benefit of others or any external influence, you are susceptible to failure, because you give your power away. You are motivated by the conditions of your external stimuli and are either driven by fear or by what others think of your journey. This is always a turbulent cycle, and worst of all, never-ending, because you can never make someone happy by the things you do. They must make themselves happy. As discussed earlier, we fool ourselves with a false sense of cause and effect. The only way to find peace of mind in your growth as a person and a leader is to know what your center of passions are and feed those desires to satisfy yourself. The rest will come. Figure out what it is you want to do and go to work.

That does not mean you become inconsiderate of others. In fact, the frame of thought advocates the opposite. When you find your passion and the way to becoming the ideal "you," you rise above the conditions and influences of those who have not done the work to discover themselves. You begin to empathize with those who are not as fortunate as you. This process can be grueling, but it can make you compassionate to those who are living in a lost world of vicious cycles with no way of understanding how to navigate out of the storm. The main purpose of authoring this book is so that you can find your way through the maze of life and become the beacon of light for others who are struggling with the storm of their lives.

BELIEF

When you focus, it gives your dream a direct path to follow. However, the necessary fuel for the mission is belief. There is a direct relationship between actions and events. We often do not see immediate results from a "cause." What I mean is that you will not see your arms bulging with muscles after your first day in the gym or witness substantial weight loss after a day of dieting. However, with time, results become apparent. The other important consideration is that correlations do not imply causation. A correlation between two things does not necessarily mean one is causing the other. One thing can be related to another, or it could simply seem that actions are related. For example, the more money I make, the fewer problems I have, or I will be happy when I achieve this particular feat. These actions seem to be directly related, but many times, do not have a cause-and-effect relationship.

The universal cause-and-effect law indicates that whatever we put out will have an effect. However, we have no idea of what effect will result from the actions we take. We control this concept

Live to Never Lose Again

through our beliefs. Our beliefs, exhibited in our responses, determine the effect any action taken or given has on us. Life is 10% what happens and 90% how you react to it. If you believe that all things which happen to you are there to hurt you, it is true. Conversely, if you believe that all things that happen to you are there to help you, then that is true. "As a man thinketh, so is he" is the best way to explain how your beliefs play a vital role in molding yourself.

Having a blind belief in a passion means that you have no disbelief. We do not know the effects our actions will produce on others, but we know what effect they will have on ourselves. An example of how belief in yourself can change the physical world is the story of Roger Bannister, a twenty-five-year-old British athlete, who, on May 6, 1954, broke the four-minute barrier for a mile run, and achieved the "unthinkable" by completing in 3:59.4. Runners had been chasing this goal since 1886, but even with the best coaches, it was considered a fact it could not be done. However, one man believed enough in himself and finally broke the mark. After years of failure, he was able to achieve the unachievable. Just forty-six days later, John Landy, an Australian middle-distance runner, broke his record with a time of 3:57.9.[11] Over hundred years later, more than a 1,600 runners have conquered the barrier. All this is because one man believed in himself first.

Storms have the effect we choose to give them. The placebo effect describes the power of the human mind and the control we have over situations through simple belief. The placebo effect is the phenomenon in which some people experience a benefit

---

[11] History.com Editors. "Roger Bannister runs first four-minute mile." HISTORY. A&E Television Networks, Revision 4 May 2020. Accessed 26 February 2023. https://www.history.com/this-day-in-history/first-four-minute-mile.

after the administration of an inactive "look-alike" substance or treatment. As an example, in 2014, psychologists conducted a migraine study using labeling of drugs affecting migraines in sixty-six people. Participants were asked to take a pill for six different migraine episodes. During these episodes, they were given a placebo or a prescribed drug called Maxalt. The labeling varied throughout the study, with some patients receiving the drug while others received the placebo. Participants were asked to rate pain intensity thirty minutes into the migraine episode, take the pill, and then rate the pain two-and-a-half hours later. Well, labeling matters! Pills labeled as Maxalt had a high rating of pain relief, even though the pills were sometimes placebo. The effect was so strong that the placebo labeled as Maxalt provided about the same relief as the drug Maxalt itself.[12] The placebo effect shows you that the mind can heal the body and did not need Maxalt.

The mind needs us to believe in our ability to accomplish and succeed. If you believe in your passion statement, you will achieve it because of your belief. It is important to not try to control the results of the ripples that form when you stir up the water. Just remember to apply your talents in alignment with your goals and focus on the daily task of fulfilling your purpose. Your results will reflect your hard work. It may not look like the results you envisioned at first, but if you look closely, you will see the reflection of your belief in your life and growth.

---

[12] Slavenka, Kam-Hansen et al. "Placebo and Medication Effects in Episodic Migraine." Science Translational Medicine. 8 January 2014. Accessed 29 August 2021. https://www.science.org/doi/10.1126/scitranslmed.3006175#:~:text=In%20a%20 randomized%20order%20over%20six%20consecutive%20attacks%2C,yielding%20 a%20total%20of%20459%20documented%20migraine%20attacks.

Live to Never Lose Again

THE PSYCHOLOGY OF FOCUS

The human mind is a powerful tool, used to evaluate everyday actions and formulate reactions. In the last few paragraphs, we have discussed how to become mindful and aware of where you are in your journey, and how to stay aware of your big picture of life. In the next few paragraphs, we will break down how the mind is conditioned and what makes us "what" we are.

Sigmund Freud, the founder of the psychodynamic approach to psychology, proposed psychoanalytic theory to explain human behavior. According to the theory, there were three levels of the mind — the id, ego, and superego. The id or instinct, which works at an unconscious level according to the principle of pleasure, operates from two kinds of instincts — biological instincts and life instincts. The id comprises our most basic and impulsive instincts, with the focal point being to satiate our desires and attain immediate satisfaction. Freud inferred that when a person's actions are driven to satisfy a need, he does not stop to think about whether the action is ethical or not.

The second level is the ego which develops from the id during infancy. The ego's goal is to satisfy the id in an acceptable way. In contrast to the id, the ego follows the reality principle and operates in both the conscious and unconscious mind, maintaining a balance between pleasure and pain. At some point, even though the person realizes that the needs of the id are unrealistic, he continues to push himself to achieve them. However, it does help to follow some guidelines after considering the ethical and cultural ideologies, thus creating a balance.

The last is the superego. It develops early in childhood and is responsible for ensuring that moral standards are followed. It operates on the morality principle and motivates us to behave in a socially responsible manner, disallowing those actions which are morally unacceptable. In short, it is the consciousness of an individual, pushing him to act ethically and adhere to cultural values, like one ideally should, while fulfilling internal desires.[13]

The objective of these definitions is to help you distinguish between "who" you are vs. "what" you have become (conditioning). Reality tells us that everything in our physical world is made real by its relationship to something or someone else. For example, heat can only exist because we compare it to cold; light exists because we compare it to darkness. The development of one's mind is highly based on the reality of those we have in our environment or choose to agree with, in terms of moral and social standards. Simply put, we all are different, share conditioned values, and social standards, and relate to situations (cause) differently according to their relevance (effect) in our lives (blueprint).

The subconscious mind is where actions go to become habits and characterize us. The conscious mind is a sponge and can choose or reject the thoughts of others. We often blindly trust those who feed us when we are young or tend to the needs of the id, so we are receptive to allowing their perceptions to seep into our subconscious. As mentioned, when discussing agendas, this is why you see many family members with the same views on topics like politics or sports, without having the slightest knowledge of the matter themselves.

---

[13] Vinney, Cynthia. "Freud: Id, Ego, and Superego Explained." Science, Tech, Math; Social Sciences. Revised 227 February 2019. Accessed 16 March 2022. https://www. thoughtco.com/id-ego-and-superego-4582342#:~:text=The%20ego%20operates%20 from%20the%20reality%20principle%2C%20which,consequences%20of%20 going%20against%20society%E2%80%99s%20norms%20and%20rules.

Live to Never Lose Again

An idea does not permeate until it sinks in or becomes a part of the subconscious. However, after years of conditioning, it is difficult to change your perspective because it is built in, and you believe what you believe. This is why letting go is so hard. The subconscious is a habitual learning tool that takes whichever thought you choose and forces it into a habit so that the body can automatically operate. Once habits are formed, it is exceedingly difficult to form new habits because the body has become familiar with the thoughts and perceptions, and standards it has learned over the last several years. Nonetheless, to bind the new you with your new conditions, this must be done.

How do we transform our conditioning? It is by renewing our minds. Conditioning is the process of training a person to behave in a certain way or accept certain circumstances. When we think about conditioning, we can refer to the strength training reference and how muscles do not grow in a day. For example, if you want to grow your biceps, you must first decide that it is the task you would like to focus on, and then identify the stimulus you need to shock your system. When lifting, you tear down the muscles and allow the shred so that you heal stronger. The repetition forces the muscle to adapt to the new stimulus and grow to meet the demand. What happens is, the conditioning of the body is done through training the muscles to react in a certain way.

There are three basic types of conditioning methods that we will explore:

1. Operant conditioning, where learning occurs through rewards and punishment for behaviors.
2. Observational conditioning, in which learning is through observing the behavior of others.

3. Classic conditioning, which is a learning process that occurs when two stimuli are repeatedly paired, and a response, which was initially elicited by the first stimulus, is eventually elicited by the second stimulus, alone.

To renew your mind, we can use one or all three of the conditioning methods. The key is to ensure that we focus on the correct stimulus and elicit the correct response. I recommend revisiting the awareness section and ensuring you know what you want to change/recondition or rediscover if you are still unaware. For the best results, it is vital to know yourself enough to understand what you need to add or improvise who you are.

Let us look at the examples of these techniques to help you understand exactly how and why they work. Operant conditioning, also known as instrumental conditioning, is often attributed to the psychologist BF Skinner. His view was simple; behavior that is reinforced or rewarded will be repeated, and behavior that is punished will occur less often. This is breaking down the law of cause and effect to its basic principles to best control outcomes. Skinner conducted experiments in 1948, using animals that he placed in a box and used a device to objectively record their behavior in a compressed time frame. In this experiment, lab rats press a lever when a green light is on and receive a food pellet as a reward. If they press the lever when a red light is on, they receive a light shock. Studies like these, although morally wrong, were common at the time. As a result of the punishment they received, they learn to press the lever when the green light is on and avoid the red light.

Observational conditioning is a form of classical conditioning but deserves a separate definition and explanation because of its distinction in the results obtained. Psychologist Alberta Bandera

Live to Never Lose Again

has been credited with research on learning through observation. In his famous Bobo doll experiment, children observed a film in which an adult repeatedly hit a large inflatable doll. After viewing the film, children were more likely to imitate the adult's violent actions, as the adults in the film had to face no consequences for their actions. Conversely, children who saw the same film where the adults were punished, were less likely to repeat the behavior later.

Classic conditioning, also known as respondent conditioning, is learning through association. The most famous example is Pavlov's dogs, discussed earlier. The ability to condition ourselves is simply a form of evolving the mind to relate to stimuli and choose our response based on the requirements in life. We are conditioned early in our lives by the environment we inherit and accept. However, we eventually get the chance to shape or reshape ourselves through the renewing of our minds. Like life storms, the conditioning phenomenon will occur, whether we choose to guide it or not.

Each conditioning method has its benefits, but I particularly prefer working with classical conditioning because it provides the opportunity for learned, quantifiable tracking of growth. The ability to quantify and count minor victories is especially important when upgrading your personality through habitual learning. Habitual reflection on our behaviors relates to us that we are becoming aware of how we invest our time, effort, and resources. A practical example of the concept that we will use moving forward is the virtue card that Benjamin Franklin used to develop character traits over time.

For a large part of Franklin's life, he carried around a card in his pocket that depicted a simple table with seven columns and thirteen rows on it. Each column on this card represented a day of the week — Monday to Sunday. Each row on this card represented one of the thirteen virtues that he wanted to work on. During the day, he might glance at these virtues a time or two to keep them fresh in his mind. At the end of each day, he would pull out a pen and go through those virtues, asking himself if he had practiced them during the day, and mark the box if he had done so. His goal was to fill in as many boxes as possible, and each week, he would start anew with a fresh blank chart. Not all the charts were identical. In fact, he had thirteen variations of the charts, which he cycled through every thirteen weeks. At the top of each variation of the card was listed one virtue, which was the main one he wanted to practice that week, along with a brief description of that virtue.

One week, he might focus on frugality, while the next week might particularly focus on temperance. He would reflect on and record his success with all thirteen virtues each day, but he would intentionally focus on just one virtue each week. As a final key part of his practice, he would review the cards at the end of each week, evaluating which virtues were successful that week, which ones were not, and which areas needed focus and improvement in his life. He would also review them as a set, and thus with thirteen cards to review, that covered three months of monitored living. A larger review like — a "quarterly review" if you will — can point to some larger patterns along your path to becoming a better person.

Over time, these virtues became increasingly ingrained in his character. He found himself naturally practicing them over time, which made him a more well-rounded and successful person and a better participant in society. He attributed his cards for being

Live to Never Lose Again

a healthy part of the success that he found in every attribute of life.[14]

Now, to break down how this condition worked. In classic conditioning, you need to identify an existing behavior that elicits a specific response. Be sure you directly link the cause-effect chain you hope to achieve. You then need a stimulus, and finally, time to associate the old response with the new stimulus. Franklin's initial behavior was that he was argumentative (strong response) with those who disagreed (stimulus) with him. His new stimulus was his virtue card category labeled "temperament," and the association was linking his accountability card and the constant reviewing and grading himself on his behaviors and reaction (response) to the same stimulus (disagreement) to track trends. As he developed trends, new techniques were used to combat the effects of the behavior until new traits became automatic or a habit.

This technique can be used for any trait or shortcoming. The challenge for most people is threefold. Firstly, most people are not aware of who or what they are. Secondly, they are not aware of what they need, because they are not aware of what cause is causing what effect. Lastly, people do not take the time to stick with change long enough to tear down old habits and build new ones. A lot of people will say they are too old to change. Here is

---

[14] Hamm, Trent. "Ben Franklin's 13 Virtues: Using One Week to Change your Life." The Simple Dollar. Revised 20 April 2020. Accessed 30 June 2022. https://www.thesimpledollar.com/financial-wellness/ben-franklins-thirteen-virtues-using-one-week-to-change-your-life/?utm_source=feedly&utm_medium=webfeeds

some personal experience. At one point, I had quite a bad teeth alignment. So, I told my wife I wanted braces, but at the same time, I was too old for them. She looked at me and said, "You are too old for your teeth to be out of line." Interesting perspective, isn't it? We are too old, at any age, for our lives to be out of line.

BREAKTHROUGH

Belief is defined as an acceptance that a statement is true, or that something exists. Our beliefs in life are so powerful but are often taken for granted because we lose or give our power away to the false reality of current situations. The power of belief was exhibited in the story of Roger Banner. He believed, achieved, and broke the barrier for so many others to achieve. The history of civilization has always had beliefs that changed the course of many lives. We view these people as heroes or saviors.

However, all of us have our personal points of success or failure throughout life. There are times when we are tested, and we all want to know how long it takes to get sick and tired of being sick and tired. When does the breakthrough moment occur? Why haven't I had it?

I do not think we fail on purpose. Paul said in the NIV Roman 7:19, "For I do not do the good I want to do, but the evil I do not want to do — this I keep on doing. Now if I do what I do not want to do, it is no longer I who do it, but it is sin living in me that does it."[15] No person is perfect. We are at war within our minds. Some

---

[15] Bible Gateway editors. Romans New International Version. Accessed 15 February 2020. https://www.biblegateway.com/passage/?search=Romans%20 7:19&version=NIV.

Live to Never Lose Again

of us have made it further along, fought more battles, have a few more scars, and are better prepared to withstand storms. Each one of us has a storm to fight. You are never alone. To never lose again, you must believe that every loss is a win. Therefore, there are only wins. Rodger Banner, Martin Luther King, Mohandas Gandhi, Nelson Mandela, and anyone else who has broken through, did one thing — they believed they could. Each of these people gave in to losing themselves to gain themselves. Every drug addict, struggling parent, or abandoned child, who has turned himself around, had a moment at his rock bottom and yet decided to believe in himself. Rock bottom is when you choose to go no further down and decide that you will change your life. Change happens when your current situation is viewed as worse than the alternatives. Breakthrough is when your *why* changes from trying to control the situation to focus on yourself.

Breakthrough moments are simply allowing change to happen through applying belief in another "why" instead of trying to force the old blueprint to work. Rodger Banner accepted that the four-minute barrier had never been broken. His breakthrough came in releasing himself from the expectations of critics, and the training regiments of others, and believing in his blueprint of how to succeed. MLK had enough hate and criticism to feel justified if he chose to pick up a stick or a brick to retaliate. His breakthrough was letting go of the mainstream eye for an eye, victory through violence concept. He was denounced by his peers and those who thought his techniques were inadequate. Nonetheless, he continued to believe in his dream, such that now, minorities across the world are living with more respect because of his notion of peace.

When you are truly sick and tired of being sick and tired, you know it because you start to make steps toward change. You can choose to change your rock bottom at any moment you feel you are not in a place that works for you. You can decide to change your why today. That does not mean the shortcomings that may live inside you will not come calling you again, but when your why is stronger than your want, which calling will become weaker and weaker. Eventually, that old calling will fade into nonexistence. The breakthrough is the change in belief of your why.

Breakthrough moments are not simply moments when we have epiphanies. Such moments are formed after a series of trials and errors until you strike gold. It is like a seed that you sow into the soil. For a seed to grow into a tree, it must get the appropriate nutrition and water to break through the soil. Your moment is coming; you do not know when, but you must have faith. You must continue to water the plant and rest in belief until your moment comes. Ask and it shall be given, seek and you shall find. *Trust this process!*

RHYTHM

Rhythm is a pattern of movement in a systematic arrangement. Have you ever been to a place listening to music and watching the dance floor as people proceeded to show off their moves? If not, the next time you go out, you should try it. Sit and watch. There is often one person who just cannot seem to find the beat. When you have rhythm, you can make up your own dance. However, if you cannot catch the beat, it is very noticeable. At times, we are like that in life. We know we can dance, but we just cannot seem to catch the beat to be in a rhythm.

Live to Never Lose Again

The rhythm of life is the direction of your life — where it came from and where you are headed to. Sometimes, we may be doing well in life, when, out of nowhere, our storm hits us and knocks us out of rhythm. We may even create these storms for ourselves when we need change. Either way, we are off track, and it can take a while to find the beat again. Rhythm is important because it helps us to become smooth and effective. If you are in a storm, going through a transition, or are merely unsure where you are, you are in a wonderful place. All you may need is to change the music. This book has taught you how to let go of any possible static and prepare yourself for the new music in your life.

Questions to ask yourself:

1. Do you believe in yourself? If not, what do you fear most?
2. Currently, where is your focus? Is it in the right place or do you need to change it?
3. What type of conditioning do you think works best for you?
4. Do you find Benjamin Franklin's virtue cards effective? Would you be willing to find your way of tracking your actions?
5. What are you sick and tired of being sick and tired of?
6. Will you take the challenge to change your habits?

Contemplate the answers to the above questions without holding back, and you will get a clear picture of whether you are where you want to be in life. If not, it will help you to think about what can be done to help you get closer to your ideal self.

CHAPTER 7

Balance

Jarvis Buchanan

WHAT IS IMPORTANT?

In the Chinese philosophical concept, the two great opposites but complementary forces at work in the cosmos are labeled as yin and yang. These forces represent masculinity and femininity, light and dark, cold, and hot, etc. The interplay of balance is believed to make up the principles guiding the universe. The reality of the matter is that we find evidence of the yin-yang balance in our everyday lives. In fact, you can find the balance or opposing forces in all facets of human experience.

We are complex creatures, and our "wires" are easily crossed when intangibles like emotions are introduced to the equation of balance. It is difficult to examine opposing forces when you are pulled into different emotional directions based on how your life and environment have shaped you. Personally, as a dreamer, I am usually resilient in pursuing audacious plans to save my view of the "wrongs" in the world. However, I am often distracted by the next fantastic opportunity to fix something before I finish the previous task I commenced. As I write, I am in the fifth year since I started working on this book. Imagine how many times I must have gotten distracted, such that I took longer to complete this one task than the desired time! At times, I feel that the "talking dog" and the squirrel reference from the movie "Up" explains my situation aptly. The dog is doing one thing and suddenly, a squirrel comes out of nowhere and he exclaims, *"Squirrel."* Immediately, he is distracted and totally focused on the squirrel.

Why does this happen? One of the best explanations I have found to help explain this experience is a blog post by Tim Urban "How to Pick a Career (That actually Fits You)." Mr. Urban does a wonderful job, using his career search model to break down the

Live to Never Lose Again

phenomena of experience, conditioning, and a multitude of other variables that influence choice. I would suggest to those who are still searching for your passion to google his work, specifically, the aforementioned blog. In his post, he indicates that society tells us a lot of things about what we should want from a career but goes on to discredit society's conventional wisdom. He chooses what he labels as a "yearning octopus" to explain the importance of finding a career, but more importantly, the importance of understanding the sheer, unimaginable extent of needs and wants that pull on you at different points in life that you must contend with during your search. For a visual perspective, picture an octopus with five tentacles, and your priority needs spread across each of these tentacles. It is understood that needs vary from person to person, but many of us have quite similar tentacles. In his example, he uses the following aspects: personal, social, moral, lifestyle, and practical. These tentacles are always in competition for your attention and *do not* get along. Your personal tentacle says, "I must achieve my potential," while your lifestyle tentacles fire back, "Yeah, but that's ruining my life!" The moral tentacle checks them both, arguing, "You are self-absorbed. We should be helping others." The social tentacle yells upon hearing the moral's philosophy, "You don't get famous by helping people!" Finally, practical just wants to know, "Anyone knows when we are getting the next check? The bills are due." He goes on to explain that each tentacle has sub needs and wants that must also be managed. [16]

---

[16] Urban, Tim. "How to Pick a Career (That Actually Fits You)." Wait But Why. April 11, 2018. Accessed 23 July 2019. https://waitbutwhy.com/2018/04/picking-career.html.

Jarvis Buchanan

If you can envision the tentacles, you better understand that balance is required to help you make decisions based on your current position within the cycle of life. These tentacles go back to the needs we discussed earlier. They are what you have defined as what you deem important. Now we need to determine how to manage expectations with so many competing squirrels.

PRIORITIES

What gets measured, gets done! If we set something as a goal, we intend to complete it. Dreamers are notorious for setting grandiose goals based on the moment. This makes us creative, but oftentimes, the goal is usually not based on the agreement of our needs. Rather, goals are based on the needs of one tentacle. I started drafting this book in 2017 with the goal of completing it in less than a year. However, I work and have a family, so that is a commitment in itself. Nevertheless, my moral tentacle told me that I needed to help others to become better. So, I dove into writing. It started off well. I was writing every day. Then, the disrupting squirrels started appearing. Since starting the book five years ago, I have founded a business as a leadership consultant, bought a hundred-year-old home, flipped it, and moved my entire family three times for my day job.

So, here I am, five years later, and the moral tentacle is still tugging to finish what I started. There are a few recommendations I have for you based on my last few years of experience. First, take some time to consider what stage of life you are in, and what you can afford to do at the time. You may be exceptionally talented, but there is a time for all things. Taking on many tasks at once only means one thing; it ensures that nothing gets done! If you

Live to Never Lose Again

feel a powerful desire or see an attractive squirrel, take a moment to evaluate what part of you wants to focus on that distraction. Does it deserve your time and effort? Does it align with the type of person you are? Does it help you to step closer to your goals? My emotions made many decisions for me, because I was on autopilot and left to wonder why I kept finding myself in the same holding pattern of starting and either not finishing, or in the case of this book, finishing much later than expected.

The problem is not so much having an idea and setting a goal as it is prioritizing the same. What makes one need more important than another? When we fail to control the narrative between tentacles, we find that we switch from one idea or a passionate thought to another, and eventually, over commit. It is important to note that dwellers are much better at managing the expectations of tentacles. Usually, they know what they want and are content working toward that goal without much change. Achievers are progressively worse as they aim to achieve too many things at once but have the dedication to complete actions for the accolades associated. However, dreamers jump around until they learn to hone their focus.

All needs want to be met and heard. Remember, attention is not something that you can give out freely. It is expensive and must be proportionate. In fact, neurological science has demonstrated that the human brain is incapable of focusing on two things at once. So, with all the banter coming from your needs, how do we determine who gets what? This is not a straightforward decision, which is why there is no cookie-cutter answer to living to never lose again. This is a deeply personal question that only you can answer for yourself.

Once you start to rearrange your behaviors based on your new priorities, you will see how jealous your other needs become.

The more you focus on your lifestyle, the more your social or personal needs feel abandoned. The more you focus on being practical, the more lifestyle must take the back seat. Can you start to see the importance of having a balance? Tim Urban indicates that the only way to control the narrative is to strike deals with the other needs. You must stroke the ego of your needs. If you have a plan to author a book, your lifestyle will suffer because you will be spending time researching, reading, and writing. Your lifestyle will feel like you are wasting away, and "You Only Live Once" (YOLO). All the other needs, whatever they may be for you, will also make the case for what is more important.

Here is where the negotiation must occur. Any newfound list of priorities for setting goals and determining which need is recognized, must come with conditions that your other needs agree to accept. You must convince your other needs of how you plan to justify spending your time, and how they will benefit overall. This is a personal negotiation with yourself. For instance, if you can tell the part of you that yearns for a grand lifestyle that it will be even better after you finish the manuscript, then you issue an IOU (I owe you) to lifestyle and plan a date to live it up after you are complete. This IOU is redeemable upon completion and *should* certainly be paid in full. You must be accountable to yourself, and you deserve it. Once you have made tradeoffs with your needs, balance can be achieved, and you can decide where your focus should go for the next phase of life.

Now, let us consider how to balance a less significant need within the focused or prioritized need. Yes, there are struggles within struggles. Continuing with the book writing example, there is indeed a moral aspect to drafting a book to help people who are struggling to make sense of all that is happening to them, but is that your true driving motive? Or is the driving motive to become

Live to Never Lose Again

well-known for contributing to society? Your motive could even be to simply make money. The priority need must be well-defined along with the baseline intent, so that you are well-grounded in completing the task for the right reason. It comes down to whether you are doing it for an internal or external reason.

Unfortunately, a moral goal driven by the wrong intent has the potential to flail out or cause more damage than harm. In many countries, innocent lives are taken by senseless mass murderers who claim to be making the moral decision to kill others based on traditional or religious principles. Religious wars, attacks on schools, churches, or social events start as moral causes inspired by the wrong wolf. To avoid the conflict, define your why and ensure that your family of thoughts is in tune with this reason. Set your intention on creating lasting value in your goal.

WILLPOWER

Willpower is the ability to control one's own actions, emotions, or urges. This control gives us strong determination which allows us to do difficult tasks. What makes one person more capable than another in having the power of will? Why are some people more disciplined than others? You may think my answer is complicated, but it is not. Those who can compromise with the many tentacles (needs) in their life to prioritize some particular goal or need are labeled as those with strong willpower. You do not need a special formula as to why you cannot get things done. If you can identify your needs and prioritize the need that supports the next goal, despite the whining of all the others, you will have a strong will. This automatically happens as you can concentrate more energy toward the purpose.

Having a strong will does not mean that if you have five needs, one must have 100% of your focus. That theory negates the concept of yin-yang. Rather, you have the ability to allocate portions of your energy to your desires as you deem fit. For example, some people may have a lifestyle that allows 80% focus on one area, which can severely stress other needs. However, stressed, this type of push can get things done quickly. Think about studying for the LSAT or GRE. You take a few weeks to shift everything else to a low roar and spend 80% of your time on studying, and 5% each on the remaining viz. lifestyle, social, practical, and well-being. You eat, sleep, and drink the test. Although not preferred, over a brief time, this type of imbalance can be beneficial in getting specific activities done. This can be applied to many life events that just take a "get it done" attitude.

In my opinion, a better alignment for consistency is a 50% focus on the prioritized need. For example, drafting a book gets 50% of my free time, while the other aspects of my life share the remaining 50%. This discounts the hours necessary for work and sleep. When I am on a mission, everyone in my life knows that I am exceptionally dedicated to completing that work. If you have other people in your life, you should share your intentions with them. Family members or friends can help you in completing your goal if they understand the balance. Here is an example of a potential conversation.

Over the course of the next few (insert time), I will be working hard to finish (goal). That means, I will be dedicating more time to this than usual, and we may not be able to continue our normal schedule until I am done. This dedication will lead us to (your goal's reason). After I reach my goal, I will have much more time, and we will be able to resume our normal schedule. You can rephrase these statements as you deem fit, but it can serve

Live to Never Lose Again

as a prototype of a conversation for those in your circle, so that they know and can support your timing and goals.

I learned in my later years that my time was something I would pay money for, bringing new value to the phrase "time is money." I would prefer paying people to do things that are not on my priority list, so that I can use my time to resource my goals. It took years to be able to afford this lifestyle, but with the proper balance upfront, this is an alternative way of managing goals and daily tasks.

Consider the following examples. I could change the oil in my car and truck, but I would rather spend my Saturday catching up on my writing or with my family. I could cook every night, but sometimes, I prefer eating out, so that I can attribute that time to other things. I could let someone give me a haircut, but I hate wasting three hours at a barber shop with my son during the weekend, so I learned how to cut hair to save time. I could pay for a gym membership, but I bought dumbbells and weights so that I can work out at home, saving time when I have more pressing matters to tend to. I could build furniture but buying it is more convenient and a time saver. In my estimation, time is one of the most valuable assets we have, and it is wise to save as much as you can for yourself. I partially agree that "time is money," whereas I fully agree that "balanced time is money." The commercial and government industries are coming around to these truths as well. You could drive to work, but those who can manage to work from home through a virtual platform will end up wasting hours on the road if they must commute to the office for the same.

Your willpower is determined by your ability to balance, divide, and conquer. To help get you off to a start, you can calculate time, just like you do anything else. It is important to know what type of time you are working with before you divvy

Jarvis Buchanan

up time to your tentacles. I use a simple weekly planner to divide where my time is going. When you start looking at time as the most valuable asset, you will start taking better care not to waste it. I challenge you to review where you spend your time. What does your balance of time look like? You may be surprised how much more time you have to put toward your prioritized goal.

I would suggest you make a weekly planner and allocate a certain number of hours to each activity conducted by you daily. For example, work, family time, recreational activities, etc. When you make such a methodical planner, you will be able to figure out that each day, there are a few hours which are available at your disposal. This is where you can break out the additional focus time. After forming your schedule, whether you have one hour or twenty hours of spare time a week, do not waste that time. Once you know better, it is up to you to do better.

Nope, it is not easy negotiating which needs get attention, but start with what you can handle. Becoming disciplined is not hard, though it is challenging, as it involves breaking apart from years of habit. The steps are what they are, and you must apply them. There is no shortcut to it. When you become conscious of your calendar, it relives the stressfulness of always being reactive and allows you to become a proactive planner. Your schedule may vary from week to week, but the key is laying out all needs and then balancing each how you see fit during the week.

PLANNING

It is critically important for you to grow into the greatest version of yourself, using fundamental planning techniques. A weekly planner gives you a fantastic way to balance your time, and

Live to Never Lose Again

you must expend the effort necessary to create balanced time commitments for all your needs. If you do not develop a set of steps or plans to progress in your life, you set into motion a vicious cycle, like what we discussed before. You continue to create storms in your life because a destination has not been set in the GPS. Each need requires a destination. Consequently, you never want to arrive at a destination, as it entails an inevitable "now what" once you reach there. Yet again, the aim is to accomplish goals, all the same. Your goals should indeed be so big that even you are afraid of them. Refer to your passion statement to start identifying your goals.

One of the popular quotes by Denzel Washington is, "A goal without a plan is only a dream." When you are sick and tired of being sick and tired, you will eventually be ready to change. There are many motivators out there who tell you to just "get it done," or "start today," or "do it now." When I knew things in my life needed to change, I paid heed to those around me who attempted to motivate me to bring that "change." The problem was not that I was not motivated (external), but I just had no inspiration (internal), and I did not know how to get it. I had no idea of exactly what I was supposed to be doing "now," what was I supposed to be "starting today."

If you have made it this far into this book, it is because you have tried and failed repeatedly, and are at a point where you are out of options. Do not worry, we all find ourselves in that phase from time to time. Trust me when I say that you are not alone, and that is why I decided to write my path out, hoping to help others find their light. We all know that we must start, and that we have unlimited potential. We have been told that hundreds of times but are still clueless. How do we do that? Start with why!

A helpful technique I like to use when searching for the broad range of areas my goals can strive in is known as the "Five whys." This concept is an iterative problem-solving process that aims to get to the root cause of an issue or problem by asking 'why' five times. First, you state the issue/problem you are facing, and then ask 'why.' Why did the issue or problem occur? Then, you ask 'why' four more times, with each question of 'why' in response to the last answer you gave. When you are able to highlight your goal, you are ready to pivot to the important topic of objectives.

Example:

1	Why do I want to become and entrepreneur?	I want financial freedom.
2	Why do I want financial freedom?	I want to be able to take care of my family.
3	Why do I care for my family's economic status?	I want to break generational barriers.
4	Why do I want to break generational barriers?	I want to be a part of positive change for my culture.
5	Why do I want to change my culture's dynamics?	*I want equal opportunity and rights for my culture.*
	You have found your way.	

Find your why and commit to the plan! If you decide to become a millionaire, the goal starts with saving $1, then $2, and so on. Obviously, there are multiple vehicles that can get you to this point, but each comes with the requirement to stop, plan,

Live to Never Lose Again

and then put the plan into action. None of us get the desired result without stopping, planning, and then actioning.

Let us understand this with a short story:

"The Axe"
Years ago, there was a woodcutter who lived in the forest.
He asked for a job from a timber merchant, and he got it.
The pay was exceptionally good and so were the working conditions.
For that reason, the woodcutter was determined to do his best.
His boss gave him an axe and showed him the area where he was supposed to work.
On the first day, the woodcutter brought down eighteen trees.
The boss was extremely impressed and said, "Congratulations! Keep up the good work."
Motivated by the words of the boss, the woodcutter tried harder the next day, but he could bring down only fifteen trees.
On the third day, he tried even harder, but he could bring down only ten trees.
Day after day, he was bringing down a lesser number of trees.
Disappointed by his performance, the woodcutter thought to himself, "I must be losing my strength."
He went to the boss and apologized, saying that he could not understand what was going on.
"When was the last time you sharpened your axe?" the boss asked.
"Sharpen my axe? I had no time to sharpen my axe! I have been very busy trying to cut trees."[17]

---

[17] Stephen. "The Story of the Woodcutter". Motivational Stories. 4 June 2012. Accessed 3 June 2018. https://academictips.org/blogs/the-story-of-a-woodcutter/.

Sharpening one's axe in this story is equivalent to planning! You cannot get so busy accomplishing your goal that you forget about planning. It is also essential, on your way to accomplishing goals, to stop, check your azimuth, and confirm you are on the right course. Living to never lose again requires you to set goals for yourself in each area of need. Each goal must be accompanied by objectives that help you stay on track. When a task gets measured, it gets done.

When you take the time to measure how much free time you have to dedicate to your needs, you can more easily develop a plan. Using a simple calendar to lay out the week is a way to make substantial improvement in your projection because it gives you an objective view of how you are spending the valuable asset of time. Consequently, you will likely have even more time to balance, because of your accountability. Following a calendar or a weekly planner can be quite tedious if you are not used to that, but it does work. Keep in mind, no week will be same, and life gets a vote on how we manage our time. However, the intent is to set your rhythm by following a plan and becoming accountable for what you do and do not do. Things change, and you must adjust to the dynamics of disruption, but with focus and determination, you will find your way.

THEN, NOW, LATER

As an avid reader and listener to some of the greatest motivational speakers in the world, I often found messages to be counterproductive. Several speakers would advocate for the need to stay in the moment because there is nothing more relevant than the "now." Others will indicate that we must be able to visualize what we want and manifest our future desires. Conversely, a few others will say you need to deal with the past before you can move forward. It can be easy to find yourself, not knowing where to concentrate your thoughts in a world filled with endless prophetic philosophers. There is truth to each of the starting points, but the part that is left out is that we are all on a different journey, and each of these ways of advancing to the next stage are necessary, but in order and balance.

As you grow to live to never lose again, recalling your past is especially important for two reasons. First and foremost, to live to never lose again, you do your dig by recalling the past. Let us face it. You did not get to where you are by magically transporting into a life you did not mold. As alluded to in the previous chapters, the dig is important. Those who are truly aware of the steps that brought them to a conclusion are far less likely to take the same steps after their awareness of the potential negative consequences. The past is our teacher and gives us instructions on how to proceed with caution so that we grow from perceived mistakes. However, it is critical that we do not spend extensive time dwelling on past mistakes. Think about the past to recall the key contributions that led you to your current situation and then let that memory go back to the subconscious. Otherwise, you will become depressed thinking about what could have, should have, or would have happened!

Secondly, the past serves as an inspiration. The beauty of memory is that you can recall negative events, which the mind has no problem doing, because they, in fact, are defense mechanisms. On the other hand, your memory bank houses many positive memories as well. These memories serve less purpose to our survival, so they tend to not be at the forefront like others. Taking a moment to close your eyes and recalling a few memories of when you had smiled or had a positive demeanor can immediately uplift your mood. If you take time during your meditations or self-care moments to bring more of these memories to the light, they can bring a burst of inspiration when you need it the most. I recommend you keep a couple of important memories for quick bursts of emotional euphoria. The past is a dangerous place to be, but when you know how to navigate and can get out of your own way, you can begin to slowly regain your self-worth.

Not to be outdone, we have our future to consider. Your mind has the same opportunities to travel with the future as it has with the past. Either you can see the future as a world of possibilities or as a world of unfathomable danger. When meditating on the future, we want to use what we know from our past to create a picture of what we want or do not want in our future. It is a blank canvas, and we apply the paint however we choose. It has not happened yet, so we could let our imaginations run wild. Many people who are not skilled in navigating their future scenarios tend to become anxious. The brain tells you that if you do this, then that will happen, or if you try this, then that will not happen. Again, it is trying to protect you. In many instances, there is truth to the scenarios, but fear of the future holds us back from accomplishing our goals. When we learn to rationalize the imminent danger and take note of the practical measures needed to avoid those dangers, we can proceed into our future with productive intent. When you can distinguish between the risks that are a real danger vs. those that are simply fear of the unknown, the future can be inspiring. This is why balanced planning is so important. It allows you to navigate out as far as your mind is willing to go, taking educated guesses based on your experience and imagination. The balance of vision from the past and projections of the future allows for the greatest experience in the present.

Live to Never Lose Again

The present is the moment that you are in right now. When we hear our greatest motivators talk about staying in the moment, it sounds so simple. Well, that is until you try to do it. Oftentimes, there is a myriad of thoughts that are trying to keep you focused on everything but now. When I stop to smell the roses, the sound of traffic reminds me that I have to pick up my son from school. When I walk down the beach, the water makes me think about the swimming lessons I should have taken more seriously a couple of years ago. When I want to enjoy a meal, I remember the dishes need to be done, but the dishwasher is broken. The list goes on and on. The present is a beautiful place, but without understanding the past and future, we will always uncontrollably bounce between realities that do not exist or pasts that cannot be relived.

Creating a balanced plan helps you remove obstructions from the present so that you can focus on what is in front of you. Once you deal with the past and use that to create an inspiring future, you do not have to continually revisit those places to worry yourself. When we fail to deal with the things that we think are looming, the brain will continue to remind us, sometimes even driving people insane. The present is a gift that can only be opened when the past and future have merged to create a safe space for you to relax your mind.

A balanced plan allows you to relax your mind. Many may think that a detailed plan for life is robotic. I would respond that anything done to its extremity can be dangerous. You do not want to be so rigid in your plan that you cannot shift, adjust, or be spontaneous. The problem that I see more often is that people are on the other side of the extreme, with no plan and allowing life to happen in its own spontaneity. The technique I offer of using the past and future to hedge the present is more of a format that you can use regardless of the situation. If you follow it closely, it can be the blueprint for living to never lose again.

DISTRACTIONS

I have saved the discussion of distraction to this point because it flows across the surface of the continuum of life and significantly impacts balance. Distraction is a thing that prevents someone from giving full attention to something else. Like all things, it has its left and right boundaries. It can be used as a technique for change or as an avenue for disaster. It is clever in disguising itself and wears many faces and needs your attention.

Have you ever wondered why humans never seem to be satisfied? I sit back and wonder why people consistently desire change, can rarely stay dedicated to a task long enough to master it, or are always looking for the next important thing as soon as they have achieved the last goal. Yes, I fit into this category as well. It is because change is the only constant in life. We desire change. Unfortunately, it takes years to understand that the grass is not always greener on the other side of that change. However, more often, it is the journey that really excites us.

Distraction may be the barking dog, the crying child, or the squirrel that appears on the branch. It is the lifestyle tentacle that pulls on your social tentacle to "get a life." It is why dreamers are never satisfied, dwellers find themselves wanting to feel a void in their lives, and achievers have problems achieving their goals. If there was an enemy to living to never lose again, I would label it as distraction. I do not promote it as an enemy, but when unchecked by the user, it has detrimental effects.

Live to Never Lose Again

Before we get into branding distraction as a horrid character in the struggle of life, let us appreciate its value. Another movie reference is the 1995 American military film, directed by Nick Castle and starring Damon Wayans, where we see distraction comedically posed as the lesser of the two evils. In the infamous "finger break" scene, a Marine Private has an arm wound and screams in agony, "Ahhh, my arm!" Major Payne (Damon Wayans) walks up and asks the Private if he wants to show him a trick to take his mind off the arm. When the Marine nods yes, Major Payne grabs his pinky finger and breaks it. Suddenly, the Private is screaming, "Ahhh, my finger!" Major Payne walks off and smirks to himself, "Works every time."

Distraction is what happens when we drift from the present into the past or the future. We distract ourselves from the moment and allow our thoughts to carry us away. It has many positive effects. It can be the sugar that makes the medicine go down. It can be used as a mental technique to avert your attention from a terribly negative event and refocus attention toward a more pleasing time. I enjoy interruptions that allow me to break contact with a task and rejuvenate myself so that when I go back to it again, I am refreshed. It is the balance to your consistency.

Unfortunately, the positive impacts of distraction are many times outweighed by the consequences of allowing it to assume residence in your life. This type of distraction is different from intentionally probing the past and balance planning for the future. This is when your mind drifts out of the moment without your approval or knowledge. These are the times when you are staring into the abyss, and people wave their hands in front of you to snap you out of it.

This diversion is what keeps you from losing that weight because of the cookies on your coworker's desk. It is why you have trouble saving money. It is why you continue to search the web or check social media to the point that it becomes an unhealthy habit. They start off harmless; a break from the norm. The problem takes shape when the body begins to crave distraction more than the task. Then, we justify spending increased time doing it to satisfy the fix. Just like anything else, it takes up residence as a habit. The space it takes up is the time or energy you allotted for something else. Similar to Rick James' famous quote I like to say, "Distraction is a hell of a drug."

We all need a break, but selecting your vice and controlling the urge should be of utmost concern when building the new life, you want. You cannot allow yourself to work consistently on a task because it will drain you. You cannot allow yourself too much deviation because unintended distraction will creep its way into your workspace. Plan your distraction timelines (breaks) as much as you can and make yourself accountable for things like work tasks or events that are scheduled so that they get done.

When dealing with your overall goals, distractions are dressed to impress and shaped to pull you off your assignment in pursuit of a shinier, new toy. Do not be misguided by the distraction wielding a shortcut to success. Listen to your mentor or read the lessons of anyone who ever did anything, and you will hear the cycled mantra that goes something like this: "I didn't quit"; "I had to stick with it"; I never gave up on it". These are the people who mastered distraction and used it as an asset vs. a liability. Sticking to the course is important to reinforce to yourself that you can complete a task. It builds you up for the bigger tasks that you will have to face. When you make plans, stick to them. The reason most people suffer defeat is because they fail to plan, or

Live to Never Lose Again

they fail to stick to the plan. A temporary defeat is not the end; it is a learning point, but for how long do you want to learn the same lessons?

Sometimes, life storms steer you off track, but it is seldom that you cannot find a way to stick to your plan. If you take time to navigate to your passion, you know that the route you selected is for yourself. Diversions are how the universe tests whether you genuinely want the thing you have envisioned for yourself. You will face many tests and will be tempted, too, but know that a distraction that is out of control is simply driving you farther and farther away from becoming the best version of yourself.

1. What are your five primary tentacles (needs)?
2. Do you have a goal set that aligns with your primary needs?
3. Are you willing to budget your life?
4. Will you stay accountable for your plans? What techniques will you use?
5. What are the vices of your choice?
6. Have some of your distractions led to disaster?
7. Are some of your distractions out of control? Can you identify them?
8. Can you use your willpower to negotiate with yourself on setting goals and fulfilling them through balance? How will you do that?

CHAPTER 8

Connections

Jarvis Buchanan

LAW OF ATTRACTION

Connections are relationships in which a person, thing, or idea is linked or associated with something else. When we make connections without the curiosity of the "why" behind the connection, it is dangerous. We discussed the masks that many connections portray in earlier chapters. They can change your life and either expedite or delay your goals. Those whom you consider close to you can direct your will toward their energy. One of my simple views of life is that if you put one person in a room with another, one person will *always* have an influence over the other, and if left alone long enough, a power exchange will eventually occur.

Connections are vital to your success because your mission or task requires the attention of others. It is up to you to choose the people who will expedite or best support your avenue to success. It is likely that you have made several connections by now and can contest the fact that everyone does not have the agenda to propel you forward. Instead, there are many who desire to use your energy to propel themselves or their agenda. There is no failure in falling prey to these people because they can be cunning, and as this book propagates, the lessons you learn will prove to be much more valuable eventually. On the other hand, you do not want recurring delays, so it is best to decide upfront as you move to this new frontier how connections work and how to make them work for you.

Some people believe in the Law of Attraction, while others do not. I am not here to describe hard limitations based on wording or descriptions that serve to divide us in our purpose of becoming the best version of ourselves. So, do not concentrate on what you

Live to Never Lose Again

have been educated on the topic as much as what the principles are teaching or guiding you to understand. The principal philosophy behind the law of attraction is that like attracts like. That means you are responsible for the people you allow to flourish in your lives. Whether that person is there to support a quid pro quo relationship where you both may thrive, or that person feeds on your energy to generate energy for their desires alone, is up to you. The law goes on to establish that your thoughts or focus have an immense impact on what happens to you.

Again, whether you believe in the law or not is irrelevant. You can simply use your context clues to bring you to a structural answer to how connections work with examples in your life. Take a moment to evaluate the relationships you considered as you did your dig. Who were the people who came along with you on your journey? If you look back, with hindsight being 20/20, who took what from whom? From whom did you take? Did you render positive energy and receive the same? Did you render positive energy and receive negative energy? Did you render negative energy and receive positive energy? Did you render negative energy and receive the same?

When positive energy is given, it increases the likelihood of a long-term relationship, and when paired with the positive energy, it promotes a healthy long-term relationship where your association is fruitful. If you render negative energy, it decreases the likelihood that the relationship will last. If that negative energy is met with the same, then you will find that the relationship will dwindle rapidly.

However, there is something in us that often attracts us to our opposites. We find sincerity in the agenda to help others, and the moral tentacles want to help those in need. If you find yourself at the wrong end of one of these relationships, know that you are tied to a draining effort. Connections that absorb your essence are not worth your time or effort. People who want help will exude positive energy and effort toward you. People who want to change will send positive energy toward you. People who want to take advantage of you will connect and drain you for as long as you allow them to do that. People headed in a direction are heading there because that is where they want to be. You may not want to accept it, but their actions are speaking loudly to life, and life responds in kind. Life introduces you to a lot of negative people. Moreover, embracing the challenge of changing a negative person almost always ends in you being more influenced by that person than vice versa. Furthermore, once that person has infiltrated your life and spread negativity in exchange for your positivity, the connection can delay your growth significantly.

MISCONCEPTION

The question is, how do we attract these people into our lives in the first place? As suggested, we find ourselves attracted to a challenge or the possibility of helping someone change. I love having the ability to help others. I am thankful that I am in the position to offer support because it is a blessing to be on the giving side rather than the asking. When considering whether to accept anyone into your new circle, you must be astute about the sincerity of people. Do not mistake a pleasing personality for a well-wisher. Many people can charm you. Do not listen to words alone. Listen to actions and believe what they say to your heart. If a person persuades you to help them, ask yourself why they need it. Is it because life storms served them bad fortune, or is it because they are looking for the next person whom they can victimize? People who are truly ready to change or looking to increase their flow of positive energy will always have actions that reflect the lifestyle they want. If their actions are not in line with your values, despite what they say, consider your peace of mind thoroughly before proceeding. Remember what it took to get you this far, and whether this person is worth the sacrifice. No one is perfect, and often, there are life happenings that put us in a bind. However, voluntary poor decisions that lead to storms are certainly just as responsible for the direction of someone's life.

There is a common misconception in understanding whether you are helping people or enabling them. There is a thin line that you must discover and not cross when aiding others. The decision goes back to the intention of the person you are trying to help. Has that person shown you that they were trying to spread positivity into the world? Remember to judge, not according to what they say, but as per the actions they take. If you review a person's history or demeanor and see that they are not adding value to society, you are enabling the wrong individual.

Enablers usually have good intentions of their own but are either blind or ignorant that they are hurting the person they set out to help. Enablers render love, money, sex, talents, and anything and everything that people want. These connections use you for your value, and when you are out, the person moves on to another to fulfill their needs. Learn to recognize the circumstances that influence your relationships, and the intentions of those influencers.

HIGGS BOSON

In the 1960s, Peter Higgs was the first person to suggest the existence of a particle that is responsible for giving mass to all physical forces. On March 14, 2013, scientists confirmed the first time they found the particle and aptly named it as the Higgs particle. In 2013, Peter Higgs and Francois Engler were jointly awarded the Nobel Prize in Physics for their discovery. Higgs boson is a particle associated with the Higgs field, which is an energy field. This field transmits mass to things as they travel through it.[18] So, what does this have to do with Living to Never Lose Again?

Think of the Higgs field as a field of snow with various kinds of people and animals traversing through the snow. In this situation, you are the particle that adds weight. Picture how much slower you would move through the snow without the aid of snowshoes. Now think about how much more difficult it is moving through this snow, holding the weight of the essentials you need for life in this situation, namely, water, food, and a tent. Lastly, think about how difficult it is when you add the weight of pulling another person and all their baggage. A person who is in the same position as you, lacking resources, can do one thing for you, weigh you down! That connection is when you both have something negative to offer one another. Know that you cannot do anything for someone else until you are able to help yourself.

Now, let us take the time to reconsider your plight. You are traveling through the snow without the right resources. You know that you can get those resources if you slow down and evaluate, plan, and prioritize. So, you decide to do that. You first drop the dead weight (other people's problems). Then, you must address your depleted essential resources. In this analogy, essential resources are the tools that this book offers: doing the dig, letting

---

[18] Gregersen, Erik. "Peter Higgs British Physicist." Britannica. Revised 25 May 2023. Accessed 12 June 2023. https://www.britannica.com/biography/Peter-Higgs.

Live to Never Lose Again

go, attaining self-worth, planning, prioritizing, etc. Over time, you replenish your resources and start to use them to accumulate the tools that make the journey easier. You need better shoes, so you plan, stick to it, and get a pair of snowshoes. You can now move more freely.

Are you prepared to take on another person's baggage? Or better still, are you willing to give someone your baggage if there is an offer to do so? To the first question, be careful not to take on too much too quickly. A few insignificant victories sometimes lead us to believe that we are ready to make connections, but it is wise to take your time until you are secure in yourself. The second question was answered by the first question. Be wise and try not to circumvent the process of your growing pains by trying to combine forces with another person to remove strain from yourself too early. It is far better to be a complete person who offers himself as a whole to others rather than a person who is incomplete and looking for someone to complete him. This is not always the case, and sometimes, we must lean on one another during challenging times, but if you can bear the pain on your own, get through it. There is a lesson to be learned in your persistence.

Never be afraid or embarrassed to ask for help! There are far too many people who are not ready to go on this walk alone. My book offers you the steps to move forward on your own, but we need you here to follow the steps! You always have options. Do not be afraid or ashamed to get help now if you need it. You are not alone.

Let us continue with our analogy. You have procured your snowshoes, made it through a blizzard or two, and are now ready to grow your tools for success. You plan and decide to get your first snowmobile. This is costly, but you know that you have the resources to manage expansion. So, you get your first two-seater. It is heavier, but having a motor propels you at such a higher speed. I think you get my drift with this analogy. You have the space to take on someone else, and their baggage too. You are complete and armed with the ability to help. Even so, just because you can do a thing, does not always mean you should do it! Check the resume before you accept applicants. I am not making a case that connections are bad but do consider that different people have different weights and can either add value or take it from your experience. Your progress is like a magnet to many who want a free ride to happy town. Be aware of your power to repel as much as you need to feel unburdened by resourcing the needs of others.

APPLIED CONDITIONING

Thus far, we have discussed the implications of external connections. But what about the internal connection between your mind and body? We have put a lot of stress on the mind to change the body and the autopilot programming. The mind is constantly telling the body that something or the other is amiss, and the body is telling the mind that you set the standards, I just fell in line. How do we get the two in agreement?

The body is a learning organism, and it does not like change. The older I get, the more I am reminded the cost of the slice of cake is one hour on the elliptical. Meditation is my preferred recommendation for making the link stick. You must choose what works best for you. However, this technique gets stuff done. For instance, you have decided that you are prioritizing opening a food truck. You know the first thing you should do is research and save money. For this plan, start with taking the body into a breakdown period. By taking this step, you exert the mind's

Live to Never Lose Again

control over the body. What worked for me in the beginning was telling the body that I was going to sit still in this funny cross-legged position for fifteen minutes, regardless of what happened around or inside me. Trust me, if you have not done this before, try it once. Your mind will be stormed with hundreds of better things that you could be doing, and the body will let you know how unpleasant this situation is for it.

However, once you get to that bell consistently, you start making the connection that you are in control of the unit that is *you*. This is a clever way of getting a small victory for yourself, and these are crucial. The feeling of accomplishment is the energy that you need to replicate when reminding yourself that you need to be disciplined in your priority. If that involves research, when the urge hits to break the plan, you have your defense mechanism in place of staying power. If you can sit for fifteen or thirty or sixty minutes, whatever challenges you, then you can certainly avoid the temptations to break contact with your research. The mind and body are meant to be together, and this is how you bring them into unison. To accomplish tasks like losing weight, trying to stop using drugs, or just wanting to save a few dollars, try meditation and building that discipline level to connect your thoughts and actions.

Another way of applying conditioning is by getting involved with projects that you have not tried before. Learn a language, paint a picture, join a bike club, get involved with a church ministry, or get a dog. These are alternatives that highlight your abilities. When you think you are consistently losing, what happens is that you do not see the wins, or the wins are too far in between, and you are unable to get the traction needed for enduring happiness to spark. These organizations help you share yourself. Learning to paint around people who are encouraging allows you to connect with like-minded people. When you get attention from others, it can help to reinforce your growth. These projects or activities also get you off the couch and stop making you feel sorry for yourself. There are several opportunities that help you give back, learn, and show off your skills. The more you learn and contribute your skills, the more the connection happens that you value. This positive loop grows substantially as you continue to accept new challenges and complete new tasks.

Around five years ago, we decided to put our daughter in dance classes because she liked dance. She was distraught the first day because she could not turn a cartwheel and cried for a while that night. She wanted to quit, but we made her go back. The next week she got better, and the next week, still better. Now, she is the lead dancer wherever we move. My guidance to her was that no one comes out of the womb as an expert. We all must learn; you are no different. Believe in yourself. There is nothing you cannot learn to do. You do not have to be the best, but you may endeavor to be. You never know unless you try. Very cliché, but if you keep trying something new, you will keep the child in you alive; your urge to learn more will do wonders to shape your personality.

TYPES OF CONNECTION

As you evolve into being a better version of yourself, you will need to understand the value of categorizing your connections and appreciating each of them for what you provide and what it provides. Not all associations are meant to be in your life as long-term investments. Some people are seasonal. Imagine yourself as a seed. You were planted, and you need three things to thrive — sunlight, water, and nourishment. The connections in

Live to Never Lose Again

our lives are the continuation of resources that offer you the vital nutrition you need. However, just as too much of one thing can hurt a plant, too little of one thing can be disastrous as well. So, timing is the key to the right networking as well as the type of associations you make.

We learn the importance of networking early in life. Everyone has a genetic affinity to their parents. Our family relationships are usually the first intimate bond many of us make. However, families are only a part of a larger group of types of "ships" viz., relationships/friendships, etc. that describe our connections. I highlight four levels of connections that you should be able to categorize each person into: acquaintanceship, friendships, romantic relationships, and family relationships.

An acquaintanceship is a person you know but is not considered a close friend. This is the person in the post office you know just enough to nod after multiple run-ins. These people may be your coworkers, associates, neighbors, or classmates. You may even strike up a general conversation occasionally, but the small bit of information you know about this person is not enough for you to consider them in any other facet than acquaintances.

A friendship is quite different. Some people treat friends better than family. A friendship is a relationship that is stronger and has an interpersonal bond. These are a few people with whom you share a deep relationship and allow into your circle of trust. This list may shrink as you grow older. Friends are people who share an exchange of energy with you. They tell you what you want to hear and are also not afraid to tell you what you do not want to hear. We share a part of ourselves with friends in exchange for a part of them.

In romantic relationships, we share a different part of ourselves. These are people who have made it out of the friend zone and have entered the intimacy zone. This is a deeper connection for some and can be considered lesser for others. We have all heard the term "friend with benefits." This is the type of connection that can be dangerous if the understanding of both parties is not aligned, as to where the boundary lines start and stop. Sometimes, even that is not enough because of the emotions involved in a sexual relationship.

Lastly, our family relationships are associations that all people are born into without question. You can love them or hate them, but we all have them. These relationships are dynamic because many similarities are attached. You often live together, you have seen a person at their best and worst, you have the same bloodline, and you have the same parenting or coding. A family connection is a type that has the power to lift you to the stars or bring you to your knees.

In keeping with the four types of connections listed here, there are three levels of connection that accompany each. The level is simply why you allow them to exist in your life today. As we begin to choose who remains constant in our lives, we still have our agendas to meet and the levels you allow set the stage for how you meet your objectives. The levels can be explained by the extent of your essence you are willing to give or receive from a person.

It is here that I get to be real with you. We all know that there are several types of relationships, but what we are not so good at is accepting the level of connection you have within that. Stop trying to force your way into a romantic relationship with someone who clearly does not want you. Stop trying to be friends with someone who wants to keep you as an acquaintance. Stop trying to turn your genetic family into close friends if they are least bit interested in the same type of relationship.

Live to Never Lose Again

The best way to give your power away is to force yourself into a connection that is out of season or that should not even have a season. If you find yourself finally getting a date with a woman or a man for whom you have lusted over for years, there is a huge probability that you would give up too much of your power to get there. Why run to people who are not running toward you? In fact, the second you start chasing something that is not for you is when you begin to lose power to that person. I am not saying that you should not be persistent in what you want, but your attempts need to be warranted and accepted. If a person reluctantly lets you into their friend zone, it creates an immediate imbalance in the energy exchange. Sooner than later, the idea of privilege and arrogance creeps in, as if a favor were done. This turns into a challenge where the unwilling person tends to think, "Let us see how far you are willing to go to sustain this new level of connection." Before you know it, you are in front of the mirror again, asking yourself who you are looking at because you do not recognize yourself for what you have become again.

During such times, you need to take a step back and consider things, taking into account all the aspects. Having read this book, you now have the knowledge and know the types of connections out there. Do not be afraid to categorize the people in your life. This is not an exercise I recommend you advertise to people. You do not need to call up anyone and notify them that you are moving them from a friend zone to merely an acquaintance. However, you need to take inventory of your vital resources and what you are getting in return. If you have family or friends, you have grown away from, do not be compelled to keep it "real" and allow the same access into your life as they had before out of some imaginary loyalty. People must earn your essence, just as you must earn theirs. The minute you see that they no longer add value to you, demote them, and move forward. I know it sounds harsh, but overall, it would make sense. I am in this to help you never lose again. You have laid your implicit trust in me by picking up this book, so in that regard, consider me to be a friend, and give the above suggestion serious thought. That is what I would tell any one of my friends.

1. What connections do you have that are weighing you down?
2. How many friends do you have?
3. Are you forcing any of your relationships?
4. Are you willing to demote such worthless relationships and move on?
5. Which tools do you need to be better resourced on this journey?
6. Are you willing to grow your resources?
7. How can you be of service to the community to show your skills?
8. Will you take the leap to sign up for something different?
9. Do you trust yourself?

CHAPTER 9

Power

Jarvis Buchanan

THE ALGORITHM

A popular cliché about asserting power over someone is to either give them what they want or hold it hostage. Throughout the initial chapters, you must have noticed the word "power" sprinkled across scenarios, examples, and firsthand experiences. That was not by coincidence. Power is everywhere. It is in the food you eat, the people you meet, your attitude and personality, even in the environment that surrounds you. Nonetheless, power is elusive. It is clever but in a cunning way. Just when you think you have it, it vanishes without leaving a trace. If you want to really grasp what power is and how to attain it, you must understand the packages in which power wraps itself and how to distinguish one type from another.

The types of power are like an algorithm. If you input the correct variables at the right time, you get the intended solution. Solutions to power problems can be understood by knowing the rules to obtain an anticipated result from a given input. These types of algorithms are difficult. In fact, they are tricky because they require you to make inferences on timing or windows of opportunities, understand the types of power, and when to apply power plays to maximize your chances of success.

People use all assets available to become successful in gaining power. During the medieval period, young women were sold to royalty or more powerful families to seal bonds that customarily ascended the poor into power or as a peace offering between rivals. Slaves have been bought and sold since ancient times. Moreover, the enslavement of others has been a successful power play for many people. When "wolves" disguised in sheep's clothing swoop in and strong-arm others to believe that they are

Live to Never Lose Again

better in some fashion or another, it sticks as the norm and results in the unfair distinctions. It is a power play that has proven itself to, unfortunately, be profitable and lucrative for many nations throughout history.

People confuse prejudice and biases made against others as the discriminator's transgression but fail to understand that it is power on the agenda of those who seek to rule you. So, they will use any means necessary to gain that power. They use any basis of differentiation like skin color, sex, ethnicity, eye color, hair color, sexuality, financial status, social status, religion, and a host of other easily identifiable discriminators to pull the wool over your eyes. In fact, it is never about the discriminator as much as it is about the power. The trickiness of power is that magical moment when the chosen discriminator becomes so prevalent that it becomes the narrative instead of the agenda of the aggressor to pursue power over you. Stay focused on your goals and beware of those distractions.

Religion has been a common discriminator for thousands of years. However, the basis of most religions are principles that require people to treat others with respect and dignity. The power lust of humankind dilutes the messages, splitting religions into many forms, factions, and faces. The concern comes when that magical transition occurs, and the focus is no longer on the values of our ancestors. We become self-righteous and demand relevancy by way of forcing our beliefs onto others. As the chess match begins, policies are written to protect and set apart the rights and interests, in keeping with the development of distinction and symbols to celebrate organizational growth and power. It was once said that the most divided time on earth is Sunday morning, and that statement has much truth. Eventually, when power is abused, greed and pride take over as people bask in their self-absorbed accomplishments.

Greed is the lust for increased power, and pride is the inability to let it go. Those who do not understand power and have the intention of bringing maliciousness to others, are often seduced into becoming arrogant and greedy. Anything in excess is dangerous, and power is no different. This is why all great nations fall and great kings are overthrown. The lack of reserve in pursuing power pushes it out of your grasp. Karma is the flow of disagreement between how power is intended to be used and how it is used. You get what you deserve when you do not respect the boundaries of power. It is not to be owned, but to be friends with those who value it.

Additionally, power has enemies who exist outside the aggressors and discriminators. Power plagues the resentful. Although these are the people who are acted upon by others, power has no sympathy for anyone who holds grudges and resentment. The formulation of resentment is confirmation that an aggressor has indeed wrestled your power away. The more you allow the actions of others to ruminate in your mind, the more power you lose. Your consumption of getting even vs. understanding the rules of how power works, gives life to a slow, blinding disease that engulfs your vision and will slowly take over your life. The weight you carry in resentment is not worth your peace, hence you must forgive the offender to free yourself.

Resent blinds the religions of the world to the greatness of unity and forces men to kill other men in the attempts to protect their private interests. Resent takes your focus off, making the decision to counter the power play and forces you to become reactive to an aggressor vs. being proactive toward your goals. When this happens, you lose power and control. Some people distract you, create false divisions, and close your eyes to the elements of power you should be focusing on getting you to the next level.

Live to Never Lose Again

Power has one more enemy, and that is, the victim mentality. Power does not save you. In fact, it avoids those who are weak and vulnerable. If you are always a victim, you no longer need to ask why you never have power. That's because you are deflecting power with your mentality. People often allow negativity to become their mantra. Power hears and sees you, and you will continue to be without it until you decide to take control of your life and make the necessary moves to regain it. Live to never lose again promotes your mental health and motivates you to make the right choices to help you move forward in life.

COMMON TYPES OF POWER

Legitimate Power is when someone is in a higher position than you, and that gives them control over you. If you are given this power, it can be taken away. A parent has legitimate power over children, being legally bound to parents. Coaches have legitimate power over players, as the title allows them to instruct players on how to play. Managers, teachers, supervisors, etc., all have legitimate power.

The advantage of legitimate power is that it creates structure. When established, this power chain of command helps to create a clear picture of roles and responsibilities. It allows you to influence from a position of oversight and make decisions based on what is best for everyone. This power helps to be efficient and shoulder decision-making responsibilities. On the other hand, the downfall is that many times, people in these positions abuse their power. The lack of satisfaction in decision-making leads others to distrust authority. In addition, the title alone does not mean you have the best candidate for the job. Legitimate power in the wrong hands can delay your progress. Be careful that those you appoint or are appointed in your life with this status deserve this power. Remember, it was given and can be taken away.

Coercive power is someone's ability to exercise authority over you by means of fear and threats, like when punishment is used as a motivation to influence a person. The fear of the threat materializing can drive decision-making and progress. You see this type of power used in conjunction with legitimate power. When a title gives you authority, many people enforce the authority by coercing others through demands and assault. These are the abusers in our communities. If you find yourself in a toxic home or work environment, it is likely that you have a coercive person in charge.

The **power of reward** is the opposite of coercive power. This power creates influence by motivating people to respond to raises, promotions, and awards. This is the positive reinforcement of behavior by offering incentives. As parents, you did this with your kids, offering money for good grades or trips to the mall for good behavior. This type of power encourages people to meet goals and apply pressure on themselves instead of others applying pressure in a less desirable manner. The power of reward is a profound influence if you know what people desire.

Expert power is when you have invested time in a subject and can now use your experience to get things done. These are people who have put in ten-thousand hours of training, research, and hard work to differentiate themselves from the pack. Doctors, lawyers, and Ph.Ds. are common examples of expert power. Once you get this type of power, people respect and trust that you earned it, and this can give you a great extent of influence. No, you do not need a title to have expert power. There are many wise men and women who exude it from life lessons alone. A lot of entrepreneurs exude it, too, especially if they are in a unique field. If you are successful, you know more about a subject area than most.

Informational power is the short-term accessibility to power through your knowledge of information that will become available to anyone. People who hold secrets over your head or try to extort you have informational power. These types of power-hungry individuals take pride in digging out information and baiting you until they get what they want. Coworkers who have knowledge of systems but do not want to share information on how to navigate or use the system seek this type of power. People who constantly want you to come to them for simple tasks hold informational power. This is the power you can easily take back if you take the time to cut out the intermediary.

Connection power is a person who has power through resourcefulness. This is the type of power you have when you know the right people. You gain influence by having the connections that matter. If you are trying to make it in an industry, it often pays to know someone with connection power. They can put you in the room with the right people. They can also take advantage of you much quicker than the other powerful types. Resourceful people are always in demand. The neighborhood guy who has a well-developed network of contacts and is always making connections or getting you the "hook-up," has connection power. These people are expert negotiators and network very well.

Referent power is the power gained by someone who is gifted with strong interpersonal and relationship skills. These are people who light up a room when they walk in and make you want to follow them wherever they go, doing whatever they are doing. These people influence you through respect and admiration. Many parents evolve from having legitimate power to referent power. When people represent the change or vision that they talk about and demonstrate solid decision-making, others begin to mimic the behavior. The leaders you hold in esteem and mentors make up this group.

POWER AND KARMA

There is a misunderstanding about power and its relationship with the proverbs: "What goes around, comes around," and "You reap what you sow." These expressions or beliefs are not aligned with attaining, sustaining, or losing power. Think of power as a weapon or a resource. It goes to those who know the rules and understand how it works. Power works above the threshold of the common phenomenon and has no respect for a person.

We were all taught that those who do us wrong will eventually get what they deserve. I think that is true, but not directly because of karma, as good things happen to bad people and bad things happen to good people all the time as well. There have been horrendous captures of entire races, stolen and treated as slaves since the onset of history and record keeping. There are multiple accounts of powerful people taking the lives of countless innocents with no justice to avail. Victims and enforcers grow old and wither away, but not before passing their power to the off springs, who understand the rules of the game and continue to deliver the same fate to the powerless.

As I pondered about power, I came to realize that things come back to people because aggressors tend to abuse power and not because bad people mystically got what they deserved. My perspective is that karma is a result of how you manage your power. Karma is not something that is happening to you or that

Live to Never Lose Again

is following you around; it is a result of your relationship with power. Turning loss into a lesson, hinges on this very point, and that is why I saved it for last. If you sow doubt and vulnerability, then you receive the results of weakness in return. If you sow confidence and strength, then you receive power in return.

The world is filled with people who believe that the next day will magically be better than the day before, or that God is going to turn things around for them as they sleep. God can do as he pleases; so, can that happen? Absolutely! However, the more I come to understand God, the less I see that happening, and the more I see him pointing me in the direction of how to turn things around for myself. We put unrealistic expectations on our faith and forget that faith without work and effort is dead. Having belief in something without action will never get you the change you want to see. Great people do not sit and wait for an opportunity to come their way. Putting life under the control of your faith alone is the last thing you want to do if you plan on living to never lose again. Your power is built on your understanding of its types, deciding what power you want, knowing how to apply it to situations, and using the resources you need to attain to make things happen. Wonder less, do more.

In fact, power seeks out the weakness of others, so it has a place to reside. In the game of power, you either have a seat at the table or you are on the menu. You decide where you are, but do not expect power to change its rules to accommodate you. You will have to take action if you want to regain your power. If you know how to wield this weapon, it will remain by your side, but the moment you lose understanding of your audience, your power will cease to exist. For this reason, ascertaining power is solely situational.

If you have been in an abusive relationship, it is unlikely your abuser is changing. Power does not give itself away. You need coercive power to combat an abuser of this sort. This power forces people to value who you are by giving them less of you or punishing their behavior with the boundaries that if that happens again, you will be finished! Abusive people do not value you. So, either they start appreciating you, or you leave point, blank, period. Be serious and get your results. Stand up for yourself and turn the tables. Where do you think people get the saying, "You don't appreciate what you have until it is gone"? When people who were weak stand up for themselves, then what is gone is the person and their power. That is karma, and that is how that cycle works. A person who abuses power over someone else loses that power, and this tends to spin people in whirlwinds and exposes their weaknesses. Notice that this transaction does not happen until a person decides on a power play and executes it. If you do not make your move, do not expect karma, faith, or anything else to save you. This relationship could go on for your entire life because the exchange is happening; power is in the presence of weakness and thriving. You are on the menu.

If you are not being heard in meetings at work, do you think that people are going to give you their speaking time so that everyone is fairly heard? Nope! So, you need expert power to demand attention. Stop asking and start demanding. Be sure not to try to force yourself into being heard by using the wrong power play. Playing the race card, gender card, or any other discriminative card to hide the fact that you do not know your stuff is coercive power, used in the wrong way, and is a recipe for disaster. On the other hand, becoming the master of your field forces people to listen. There are some instances when you will find those who are hardheaded, but it is only a matter of time

Live to Never Lose Again

before they are exposed, because your knowledge is undeniable as an expert, and no one can take that power away. You are at the table.

You want to climb your way up in a world of giants and may need to become a connected power player in situations like these. If you are not well-known, become the person who knows the person in power. When I was a lieutenant in the Army, fresh out of the Officer Basic Course, I had the opportunity of becoming an Aide-de-Camp to a General Officer. It is a prestigious position, but it is challenging for young officers. You are the personal assistant for high-ranking officials and in-charge of all activities for that position. Only a few are chosen for this job because it takes a particular personality to deal with arranging meetings with people who are ranked higher than you, or explaining why senior staff members cannot have their way in certain situations. It is a delicate position and is not for everyone, because most people do not like the perception of being in a position where the hours are long, and the operation tempo is always high. This position was the best position of my career. Yes, it sucked at times. However, I came to know everyone. I was the man next to *the* man. I was the resource for getting what you needed to get done. It helped to put my name in circles it would have never been in before and it has helped me ever since that point. If you are not being heard, take the job that no one else wants, and do the things that no one else will do. Build a network that no one has built. Bridge the gaps that are obstacles for your team. Make yourself relevant through your actions. Watch how things change, and how power comes to you. You are at the table.

These were just a few examples of how to recognize your situation and decide to pivot as required to regain your power. The most important thing for you to do in situations where you feel vulnerable is to understand who has your power, the tactic they are using to keep it, and how you need to change to get it back.

Competitive Power

In defense, no one wants to give ground to an opposing force, whereas, in offense, the objective is to seize the initiative and take ground. So, what happens when your offensive power play meets the defensive power play? What happens when a new technique collides with an existing technique? It results in a power struggle. One of you will victor as being stronger than the other. Keep in mind that power applied in the wrong situation or not tailored to a particular audience is temporary. Thus, crowning a victor comes down to who has chosen the right power play for the game.

VIGNETTES: EXAMPLES OF POWER PLAYS

The next few vignettes will provide comparisons of types of power in competition with one another. These scenarios will help to shape your historical perspective of how power plays were either well-managed or mismanaged, leading to power shifts. You may not be able to use the same power counter moves to combat your power disadvantages; however, this gives you an idea of how power communicates in the language that you can understand, if you stop to listen.

A. Referent Power vs. Coercive Power

The game is about freedom, and the players are the British and Mahatma Gandhi. Gandhi was born in 1869. He was a Indian

Live to Never Lose Again

nationalist leader and a prophet of nonviolence. For most of his life, he fought against injustice by using nonviolent tactics. Let us have a look at the timeline which shall help us to understand the ideologies of Gandhi and the type of power he used to motivate millions of Indians to gain independence from two hundred years of British rule.

1906-1915

"In 1906, a discriminatory law is passed in the Transvaal region of South Africa, forcing all Indians to register with the provincial government or else face punishment. Under Gandhi's leadership, the Indian community takes a pledge to defy the law and to suffer all the penalties resulting from its defiance. This practice becomes known as satyagraha, a technique for redressing wrongs through inviting, rather than inflicting, suffering, for resisting adversaries without rancor, and fighting them without violence. Gandhi was frequently jailed during the ensuing years. Thousands of other Indians are imprisoned, flogged, or shot. The law is eventually abolished, though racial discrimination in the country continues. Gandhi returns to India in 1915.

1930-1931

Gandhi leads tens of thousands of Indians on a 240-mile (385-kilometer) march to the sea to collect their own salt. The march is a protest against a British tax on salt and results in 60,000 people being arrested. In 1931, the British viceroy and Gandhi sign an agreement (the Gandhi-Irwin Pact), marking the end of a period of civil disobedience in India against British rule. The pact involves Gandhi pledging to give up the satyagraha campaign and the British viceroy agreeing to release all those who had been imprisoned and to allow Indians to make salt for domestic use.

1932

Under a new viceroy, Gandhi is imprisoned again. While in prison, he fasts to protest the British decision to segregate the so-called untouchables (the lowest level of the Indian caste system) by allotting them separate electorates in the new constitution. The fast causes an emotional upheaval in the country, and the British agree to change the policy.

Gandhi was an artist in recognizing the presence and power of the people and encouraging influence that connected to the masses. To him and many others, timing and opportunity created the opportunity for power shifts to occur. Gandi continued to demand for independence though abiding by their core principle of non-violence. During World War II, Gandhi demanded immediate independence in lieu of aiding Britain in the war. His demand was met with imprisonment for two years. This enraged the Indians even more. With strategic planning and under the guidance of eminent leaders, India was finally able to gain independence on August 15, 1947. The Indian Independence Struggle has been exemplary as to how referent power can win over coercive power, despite all odds against them". [19]

B. Coercive power vs. Informational power

The year is 1917, and President Woodrow Wilson desperately wanted to avoid getting involved in WW1. His intent was to preserve American neutrality. On many occasions, Germany had attempted to coerce Mexico to insight war with the United States of America. The Germans thought that an attack by Mexican

---

[19] The Editors of Encyclopedia Britannica. "Mahatma Gandhi Timeline." Britannica. Accessed 23 February 2023. https://www.britannica.com/summary/Mahatma-Gandhi-Timeline.

Live to Never Lose Again

forces would slow down any support the United States provided to European Allies. Several failed attempts to insight a U.S. vs. Mexico War using coercive tactics did not work, but the use of informational power forced President Wilson and the U.S. into action.

The message came in the form of a coded telegram dispatched by Arthur Zimmermann, the German foreign secretary, to the German ambassador in Mexico. It was a proposal by the German military for an alliance with Mexico and Japan in case the United States declared war on Germany. The message was intercepted by the British and passed on to the United States; its publication caused outrage and contributed to the U.S. entry into World War I. The decoded telegram was as follows:

"We intend to begin on the first of February unrestricted submarine warfare. We shall endeavor in spite of this to keep the United States of America neutral. In the event of this not succeeding, we make Mexico a proposal of alliance on the following basis: make war together, make peace together, generous financial support and an understanding on our part that Mexico is to reconquer the lost territory in Texas, New Mexico, and Arizona. The settlement in detail is left to you. You will inform the President of the above most secretly as soon as the outbreak of war with the United States of America is certain, and add the suggestion that he should, on his own initiative, invite Japan to immediate adherence and at the same time mediate between Japan and ourselves. Please call the President's attention to the fact that the ruthless employment of our submarines now offers the prospect of compelling England in a few months to make peace.
signed, ZIMMERMANN".

In this example, the timing was indeed everything. Had the British not intercepted the Zimmerman note, the U.S. might have had a prolonged entry into WW1 or would have never entered at all. The power of information is a deadly weapon. [20]

C. Expert Power vs. Legitimate Power
Katherine Johnson Biography | NASA

"Being handpicked to be one of three black students to integrate West Virginia's graduate schools, is something that many people would consider one of their life's most notable moments, but it's just one of the several breakthroughs that have marked Katherine Johnson's long and remarkable life. Born in White Sulphur Springs, West Virginia, in 1918, her intense curiosity and brilliance with numbers vaulted her ahead by several grades in school. By thirteen, she was attending the high school on the campus of historically black West Virginia State College. At 18, she enrolled in the college itself, where she made quick work of the school's math curriculum and found a mentor in math, professor W. W. Schieffelin Claytor, the third African American to earn a Ph.D. in mathematics. She graduated with highest honors in 1937 and took a job of teaching at a black public school in Virginia. Katherine and her husband decided to move the family to Newport News, Virginia, to pursue the opportunity, and Katherine began work at Langley in the summer of 1953. Just two weeks into her tenure in the office, Dorothy Vaughan assigned her to a project in the Maneuver Loads Branch of the Flight Research Division, and Katherine's temporary position soon became permanent. She spent the next four years analyzing

---

[20] The Editors of Encyclopedia Britannica. "Zimmerman Telegram". Revised 27 May 2023. Assessed, 18 February 2023. https://www.britannica.com/event/Zimmermann-Telegram

Live to Never Lose Again

data from flight tests and worked on the investigation of a plane crash caused by wake turbulence. As she was wrapping up this work, her husband died of cancer in December 1956.

In 1962, as NASA prepared for the orbital mission of John Glenn, Johnson was called upon to do the work that she would become most known for. The complexity of the orbital flight had required the construction of a worldwide communications network, linking tracking stations around the world to IBM computers in Washington, Cape Canaveral in Florida, and Bermuda. The computers had been programmed with the orbital equations that would control the trajectory of the capsule in Glenn's Friendship 7 mission from liftoff to splashdown, but the astronauts were wary of putting their lives in the care of the electronic calculating machines, which were prone to hiccups and blackouts. As a part of the preflight checklist, Glenn asked engineers to "get the girl" — Johnson — to run the same numbers through the same equations that had been programmed into the computer, but by hand, on her desktop mechanical calculating machine. "If she says they're good,'" Katherine Johnson remembers the astronaut saying, "then I'm ready to go." Glenn's flight was a success and marked a turning point in the competition between the United States and the Soviet Union in space".[21]

Katherine Johnson demanded her respect and superseded labels. Her expert opinion garnered the trust and acknowledgment of her peers. She took advantage of the power of knowledge and became an expert who had the potential to challenge the legitimacy of computers over the genuineness of human expertise.

---

[21] Sheetly, Margot. "Katherine Johnson Biography." From Hidden Figures to Modern Figures. Revised 24 February 2020. Assessed 12 August 2022. https://www.nasa.gov/content/katherine-johnson-biography.

Granted, these are larger-than-life examples of power shifting at the macro level, but rest assured, it works the same way on a smaller scale. I could go down a laundry list of personal examples, but the truth is that you must find your way with the variables in play. Power plays exist all around us. If you choose to learn the algorithm and apply the appropriate variables, you have all the tools you need to succeed. Know your power and take hold of it.

Whatever you do, do *not* take the lessons of power personally. **Power** has been around since there have been men to desire it, offering herself to those who are willing to learn and understand her ways and will be around well after we are gone. It works for those who appreciate the value of power and are willing to follow the guidelines to attain and hold on to her beauty. If you attempt to hold her too tight, the sting of rejection can be costly, or if you allow her too much space, she could be lost forever. However, if you listen to her actions and pay attention to her moves, then you have befriended the queen of all queens.

The queen lives with her king, **Hope**. Without hope, you will not be able to access the queen. Hope has triggered every action since the beginning of time. The belief that it can be done is the single most important lesson that you should take from this book. Either it has been done before or you can be the first to do it, but hope is necessary to make anything happen. Your hope is what allows your faith and belief to move to a knowing that you will attain what you set out to achieve. Knowing is the inevitable truth that you have what you want, and it is a matter of time. Hope inspires action, and to act, you will need Hope's son, a prince named **Focus**.

Focus is the action behind our hope. It is your unadulterated attention to your intention. It is the work that you put in to get yourself past where you are and into that best version of yourself.

Live to Never Lose Again

How focused can you be without distraction? How focused will you become in your quest to become a part of this Royal Family? When you are ready, I can assure you that you are welcome to have a seat at the "live to never lose again" table.

Here are a few questions to ask yourself:

1. Who has power over you in your life?
2. Who do you have power over?
3. What do you want to have power over?
4. Can you use the definitions of the types of power to devise a plan for how to ascertain the power you seek?
5. Are you willing to stay committed to the algorithm you create for power once you understand how to get what you want?
6. Do you see how the abuse of power has detrimental impacts?
7. Will you agree to never abuse your power?

Visit www.ldrpsy.com for, tailorable, tools and tactic for the next step of your journey. You will find:

- The *questions* referenced at the end of each chapter.
- An example *budget time calendar* to help you take charge of your time.
- A personal *passion questionnaire* to assist you in examining your purpose.
- A *bonus offer* to further support your next steps toward Living to Never Lose Again.

Epilogue

Thank you for taking time to finish reading this book. I hope it adds value to your life. The intent is purely to give people a detailed understanding of awareness and to provide a strategic model to start the plan for your journey to the best version of yourself. Life is hard, but it is also good. It can be unforgivingly tough at times, but do not forget your value and appreciate your worth. The preciousness of the gift of life is a wonder; how to use it is entirely your choice. Be diligent in your endeavor to succeed, and one day, you are sure to discover the fullness of your worth. Be sure to stick around through your tests until that happens. Being honest with yourself, discipline, and challenging work are tools which help you surmount huge obstacles in life. By now, you must have understood through the numerous examples I have mentioned in the book that those who withstood the storms of life, managed to accomplish their goals, and so can you. Remember that you were selected against billions of others to be in this moment and were uniquely shaped and formed to be brilliant. So, let brilliance be your choice.

Before we end this book, I would like to reiterate that you always have options. You are never trapped, and you are never alone. We all have times of confusion, disruptions, and chaos in our lives. However, you also need to remember that by design, the dark times are magnified to increase your strength and to

Jarvis Buchanan

help you grow. Never give up on yourself, because once the sun shines again, you will appreciate its beauty that much more. Take advantage of the techniques and tips that I offered and implement what you can. I thank God for you and pray you find your way.

Thank you,
Jarvis Buchanan

References

1. Dr. T. Collins Campbell and Thomas M. Campbell, The China Study,1st. Dallas, TX: BenBella Books, 2006, 233.

2. Dr. T. Collins Campbell and Thomas M. Campbell, The China Study,1st. Dallas, TX: BenBella Books, 2006, 233.

3. Merriam Webster's Collegiate Dictionary. 12th ed. Springfield, MA: Merriam-Webster, 2003. Also available at http://merriam-webster.com/.

4. Phillippa Lally, "How are habits formed: Modeling habit formation in the real world". *European Journal of Social Psychology* (2009) accessed June 12, 2023 ehttps://onlinelibrary.wiley.com/doi/abs/10.1002/ejsp.674.

5. Kawasaki, Guy. "The Meaning of Meaning." March 1st 2015, accessed 5 May 2023, https://guykawasaki.com/the-meaning-of-meaning/.

6. Cherry, Brenda. "What Is Classical Conditioning in Psychology? How It Works, Terms to Know, and Examples.", Theories Behavior Psychology. revised 5 May 2023. accessed 12 June 2023. https://www.verywellmind.com/classical-conditioning-2794859.

7. Kenton, Will. "Zero-Sum Game Definition in Finance, With Example." Futures and Commodities Trading Strategy and Education. Revised 16 August 2022. Accessed 12 February 2023. https://www.investopedia.com/terms/z/zerosumgame.asp#:~:text=In%20financial%20markets%2C%20futures%20and%20options%20are%20considered,then%20the%20wealth%20is%20transferred%20to%20another%20investor.

8. McCallister, Nate. "Price's Law – What It Is and How to Leverage It to Change Your Business." Entreresource. 21 June 2021. Accessed 14 May 2022. https://entreresource.com/prices-law/.

9. Cherry, Kendra. "Action Potential and How Neurons Fire." Theories Biological Psychology. Revised 19 November 2021. Accessed 15 October 2022. https://www.verywellmind.com/what-is-an-action-potential-2794811

10. Bruce Feiler, "Life is in the Transitions: Mastering Change at Any Age." (London, England, Penguin Press, 2020), Retrieved 15 January 2022. from https://www.audible.com.

11. History.com Editors. "Roger Bannister runs first four-minute mile." HISTORY. A&E Television Networks, Revision 4 May 2020. Accessed 26 February 2023. https://www.history.com/this-day-in-history/first-four-minute-mile.

12. Slavenka, Kam-Hansen, Moshe Jabubowski, John M. Kelley, Irving Kirsch, David C. Hoaglin, Ted J. Kaptchuk, Rami Burnstein. "Placebo and Medication Effects in Episodic Migraine." Science Translational Medicine. 8 January 2014. Accessed 29 August 2021. https://www.science.org/doi/10.1126/scitranslmed.3006175#:~:text=In%20a%20randomized%20order%20over%20six%20consecutive%20attacks%2C,yielding%20a%20total%20of%20459%20documented%20migraine%20attacks.

Live to Never Lose Again

13. Vinney, Cynthia. "Freud: Id, Ego, and Superego Explained." Science, Tech, Math; Social Sciences. Revised 227 February 2019. Accessed 16 March 2022. https://www.thoughtco.com/id-ego-and-superego-4582342#:~:text=The%20ego%20operates%20from%20the%20reality%20principle%2C%20which,consequences%20of%20going%20against%20society%E2%80%99s%20norms%20and%20rules.

14. Hamm, Trent. "Ben Franklin's 13 Virtues: Using One Week to Change your Life." The Simple Dollar. Revised 20 April 2020. Accessed 30 June 2022. https://www.thesimpledollar.com/financial-wellness/ben-franklins-thirteen-virtues-using-one-week-to-change-your-life/?utm_source=feedly&utm_medium=webfeeds

15. Bible Gateway editors. Romans New International Version. Accessed 15 February 2020. https://www.biblegateway.com/passage/?search=Romans%207:19&version=NIV.

16. Urban, Tim. "How to Pick a Career (That Actually Fits You)." Wait But Why. April 11, 2018. Accessed 23 July 2019. https://waitbutwhy.com/2018/04/picking-career.html.

17. https://academictips.org/blogs/the-story-of-a-woodcutter/

18. Gregersen, Erik. "Peter Higgs British Physicist." Britannica. Revised 25 May 2023. Accessed 12 June 2023. https://www.britannica.com/biography/Peter-Higgs.

19. The Editors of Encyclopedia Britannica. "Mahatma Gandhi Timeline." Britannica. Accessed 2 February

2023. https://www.britannica.com/summary/Mahatma-Gandhi-Timeline.

20. The Editors of Encyclopedia Britannica. "Zimmerman Telegram". Revised 27 May 2023. Assessed, 18 February 2023. https://www.britannica.com/event/Zimmermann-Telegram

21. Sheetly, Margot. "Katherine Johnson Biography." From Hidden Figures to Modern Figures. Revised 24 February 2020. Assessed 12 August 2022. https://www.nasa.gov/content/katherine-johnson-biography.

About the Author

Jarvis Buchanan is a twenty-year Army Veteran with a natural passion for motivating others. His military career is only exceeded by his passion for helping youth and adults become the greatest version of themselves. Armed with a bachelor's degree in psychology and a master's degree in leadership and management, he established LeadershiPsych in 2022. "Live to Never Lose Again" is a part of a larger whole under this company. LeadershiPsych is an online learning platform that incorporates the lessons learned from "Live to Never Lose Again" by dividing them into lesson plans for 90 days of accountable, continuous education toward achieving entrepreneurial aspirations. Jarvis believes that it is possible to mold personal passions into your tool to combat life challenges. LeadershiPsych specializes in helping you manage the only consistent thing in life — change. Together, we break habits, thought patterns, and condition a new mindset, centered around your entrepreneurial passion.

In addition, he has authored three children's books titled "I Dream in Color". All three are motivational tools, inspired by true events, military history, and his personal passion to inspire change, and is a fun way of educating children about history.

Jarvis desires to be the change that he so much wants to see in a world of uncertainty. His light shines brightest when he can influence, encourage, and support those in need.

Printed in the USA
CPSIA information can be obtained
at www.ICGtesting.com
LVHW050606041123
762866LV00079B/2814